Maximize Your Investment:
10 Key Strategies for
Effective Packaged Software
Implementations

Accelerate packaged (COTS) software
implementations, increase returns on investment,
and reduce implementation costs and customizations

Grady Brett Beaubouef, PMP

PAM,

Sorry for the
challenges with the
KINDLE ebook. Thank
you for supporting my
efforts!

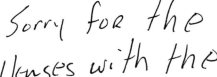

BIRMINGHAM - MUMBAI

Maximize Your Investment: 10 Key Strategies for Effective Packaged Software Implementations

First published: December 2009

Production Reference: 1091209

Published by Packt Publishing Ltd.
32 Lincoln Road
Olton
Birmingham, B27 6PA, UK.

ISBN 978-1-849680-02-8

www.packtpub.com

Cover Image by Tina Negus (tina_manthorpe@sky.com)

Credits

Author
Grady Brett Beaubouef, PMP

Reviewers
Bob Cutler, PMP

Charles J. Miller, PMP

Chris Papesh

Acquisition Editor
James Lumsden

Development Editor
Amey Kanse

Technical Editor
Ajay Shanker

Indexers
Hemangini Bari

Monica Ajmera

Editorial Team Leader
Akshara Aware

Project Team Leader
Priya Mukherji

Project Coordinator
Leena Purkait

Proofreader
Dirk Manuel

Graphics
Nilesh R. Mohite

Production Coordinator
Adline Swetha Jesuthas

Cover Work
Adline Swetha Jesuthas

About the Author

Grady Brett Beaubouef, PMP is a project manager and solution architect for enterprise packaged software solutions. Brett has over fifteen years of packaged software implementation experience across several implementation roles including Project Manager, Solution Architect, Functional Lead, Technical Lead, Business Analyst, Software Quality Analyst, and Trainer. Brett also worked in a thought leadership role for the #1 business software maker, focusing on implementation methodologies, project assessments, and accelerated implementation services. Brett has a B.S. in Computer Science from LSU and is both a Project Manager Professional (2004) and a Certified Information Systems Auditor (1995).

Acknowledgement

My Customers

I have been blessed to work with many outstanding customers on their packaged software implementations. A special thank you to those of you who made an investment in me to help me better understand your business, and who taught me how to be a better consultant/partner.

My Colleagues

I have had the great fortune to work with many outstanding people who have shared their experience with me, guided me, and supported me during my great adventure in writing this book. A special thanks to Bob Cutler, Charles Miller, and Chris Papesh for their expert insight and feedback. Thank you to Sheila Cepero for helping me find the right publisher.

My Publisher

I would like to say that I am a mature, polished author and it was easy to work with me—but that is not quite true. I would like to say thank you to Packt Publishing for their patience, understanding, and guidance as I took my first dive into publishing. Thank you James, Priya, Leena, Amey, and Ajay for your partnership!

My Family

My greatest achievement! To Lisa, my wife who loves me and is my best friend. To Samantha my daughter—never be afraid to lead with your heart!

My God

To God for giving me the ability, Jesus for giving me the passion and His Spirit for giving me the encouragement to continue with this book in spite of my limitations.

About the Reviewers

Bob Cutler, PMP has over twenty five years of project management experience in both the private and public sectors. He has lectured internationally on project management and is a contributor to the Project Management Body of Knowledge on the topics of time management and cost management. He has successfully managed multi-million dollar Information Technology projects in California for several large public agencies. All of those projects were completed on schedule and within budget.

One of Bob's specialties is project remediation. He has successfully turned around failing projects for multiple clients on two continents. His process involves focusing on the project's goals, instilling trust, and restoring morale. Client satisfaction ratings at the end of those projects have always been excellent.

Bob has been involved with national and global project management offices for two multinational corporations. On those engagements, he was responsible for identifying and/or developing tools and best practices for project managers across the organization. He has also delivered advanced training on scheduling, quality, and risk management, and was a key contributor to the development and modernization of his clients' project management methodologies.

Charles J. Miller, PMP is a Certified Project Management Professional with over ten years experience in managing high-performing teams in the computer manufacturing, software, and telecommunications industries. He has spent most of his career on large-scale Oracle ERP implementations, but has also been a leader of software and web development teams, financial process improvement initiatives, and general technology implementation projects. Charles lives in Denver, CO and currently works as a Professional Services Consultant for a Software-as-a-Service company that provides channel sales solutions to global technology manufacturers.

Chris Papesh serves as CEO of Open Healthcare Analytics, leading the design and implementation of open source data warehousing software for healthcare providers. He has over twenty years of experience in all phases of the design, development, implementation, and project management of computer business systems. Chris has been a leader in the Oracle, PeopleSoft, and Data Warehousing communities. Chris served as Technology Director for PeopleSoft Corporation and Oracle Corporation, and has led national Business Intelligence and Data Warehousing consulting practices. Chris served as an Assistant Vice President for Carnegie Mellon University and Director of Financial Services for the University of California, and has spent more than 10 years as a part-time university instructor.

I wish to thank Brett for his thoughtful analysis and case histories, and stories of real teams in action implementing complex enterprise software.

Table of Contents

Preface

Starting back in the 1980s, Commercial Off-The-Shelf (COTS) or packaged software such as Enterprise Resource Planning (ERP) applications were deemed to be the panacea to business pains caused by operational inefficiencies and disjointed applications. This resulted in an exponential growth in the ERP marketplace. To quickly meet this demand, ERP vendors and implementation partners used existing Software Development Lifecycle (SDLC) methodologies like Waterfall as the de facto implementation approach for ERP. This quick-fix decision resulted in an approach that was not effective for packaged software implementations, and that caused several issues. These included:

- Unnecessary requirements being captured (i.e., requirements gathered based upon limitations of existing systems).
- Requirements validation happening late in the implementation cycle.
- Highly-customized solutions that left customers with the same or even more challenges.
- Unrealized business results and benefits because the implementation focused only on the software.

In my fifteen years of implementation experience, I have been fortunate to play the roles of Information Technology (IT) auditor, functional consultant, technical analyst, programmer, Data Base Administrator (DBA), business analyst, solution architect, and project manager. Through my experiences, I have formed the following observations:

- Customers are more concerned with implementing successful business solutions, not just installing software products and technologies.
- Leading implementation methodologies are not focused on all of the components of a business solution. These components must work in unison in order to generate business value.
- Every business solution implementation is a "point-in-time" solution.
- Flexibility in a business solution starts with a flexible implementation approach.

Over the past two decades, the ERP industry has made incremental improvements in the implementation of enterprise business software—specifically, in the areas of implementation tools like industry-specific preconfigurations, online software product setup assistants, and data conversion tools. These improvements provided value from an efficiency perspective, however, there was little accomplished to address how to make ERP implementations more effective at delivering business value.

The strategic value of purchasing ERP—or any—packaged software is to reduce the customer's Total Cost of Ownership (TCO) for their existing business system, as well as allowing the customer to focus on more strategic objectives. The customer would pay some type of maintenance fee to the software vendor, who would then provide support and upgrades. In theory, this approach seems mutually beneficial to all players. However, the reality is that packaged software customers have not been able to experience the lower TCO due to the following:

- Initial implementations are taking longer and cost more than originally planned.
- Software upgrades are more costly because implementation approaches focus on turn-key, point-in-time business systems, and not on putting the customer in the best position to leverage future COTS software upgrades.
- Customers were never given the complete holistic approach needed to optimize their new enterprise business solution.

If you think I'm only speaking of software, then I suspect that you are one of the many people who believe that ERP has been a tremendous disappointment.

Vision of the future

To get to a point where we can get customers to experience the full benefit of their ERP investment, we must EVOLVE our way of thinking on ERP implementations—or any packaged software implementation. The ideal COTS software implementation approach would focus on maximizing the "out of the box" value that packaged software can provide to a customer. The implementation approach would naturally filter out requirements that did not provide quantifiable business value, and keep the focus on the customer's value-added strategic requirements. There would be no need for post-production support provided by implementation partners because the customer would be confident in supporting their business solution. Upgrades are done in weeks instead of months or even years. The project team would have a common language (technology, business, software) that they could speak, in order to collaborate effectively. Validation of business requirements would happen early and often. Organizational change would be manageable because it would be minimized. Business sponsors and end users would see and touch the business solution months before end user testing. Individual project team meetings would generate more decisions and less action items. Implementation costs associated with packaged software would be less than the normal—which is four to six times the cost of the software—because implementation partners would spend more time enabling customers to lead, versus performing staff augmentation. Customers would be left with an actionable roadmap to further leverage packaged software functionality as their business model evolves.

The implementation of packaged software is more than just installing and configuring software: it is the implementation of a business solution. A business solution is far more than just the software. Today, the majority of implementation approaches are guilty of focusing on one of the obvious components (products and technologies), or all of the components separately but not in unison throughout the implementation lifecycle.

Purpose of this book

The main objective of this book is to discuss an approach to implementing COTS software that will maximize the total ownership experience. This book focuses more on the art of effectively applying implementation methods for COTS implementations. As the IT market continues to move to a component-based software development paradigm, using available enterprise-wide software packages and "best-of-breed" applications in the marketplace, I believe this approach will become more relevant.

This book also serves as a challenge to implementation partners and internal Information Technology (IT) organizations that support packaged software implementations. This book will address the change in approach and direction we need to take as we evolve packaged software implementations to the next level, and generate greater business value for our customers. I will discuss different implementation methods and demonstrate how these perceived competing approaches can actually complement one another—it's just a question of identifying the appropriate level, and knowing when to apply these different disciplines. This book will identify the major factors that must be considered when defining the appropriate implementation approach.

I will also spend time in addressing packaged implementation perceptions and myths, in order to better define expectations of a COTS implementation. I firmly believe that business process methodologies like Business Process Management (BPM), Business Process Re-engineering (BPR), Lean, and Business Quality (e.g., Six Sigma) can and should intertwine within a COTS implementation lifecycle.

Out of scope for this book

The purpose of this book is not to rehash ideals and concepts that are present in the general mindshare of customers, implementation partners, and specialists regarding a successful implementation. This book will not define a new implementation methodology—there are plenty of methodologies out there, with their inherent advantages and disadvantages. This book will provide guidance on determining how to appropriately apply methodologies for packaged software implementations.

What this book covers

Chapter 1 is an introduction, covering the ten principles for implementing a business solution.

Chapter 2 covers how to ensure that packaged software implementations focus on value-added business results.

Chapter 3 covers how to effectively create alignment with implementation partners by performing a formal knowledge transfer of the existing business solution.

Chapter 4 outlines a key approach that implementation partners can take, in order to ensure long-term success for their customers.

Chapter 5 discusses a best implementation practice for gathering and validating business requirements for packaged software.

Chapter 6 discusses how to select and apply relevant disciplines when supporting the customer's unique implementation.

Chapter 7 discusses a best implementation practice for the initial implementation of the packaged software.

Chapter 8 discusses a software change strategy for COTS software that will minimize potential risks and maximize opportunities for additional software value.

Chapter 9 outlines the negotiation strategy required for implementing COTS software that will maximize the ownership experience.

Chapter 10 defines a new project role that will increase the success of the business solution implementation.

Chapter 11 focuses on effective knowledge generation.

Chapter 12 revisites the principles expanded upon in this book, and discuss how to evolve our strategy for implementing packaged software.

The *Appendix* is a summary of challenges.

Who this book is for

This book is aimed at enterprise architects, development leads, project managers, business systems analysts, business systems owners, and anyone who wants to implement packaged software effectively. If you are a customer who is looking to implement packaged software in the future, then this book will provide you with a strategy for maximizing your investment. If you are in an internal IT role and you find that your internal software development methodology doesn't quite work for an "off-the-shelf" business software package then this book will provide you with a perspective on how to adjust your approach. If you are an implementation partner looking to minimize the blood, sweat, and tears shed when implementing packaged software, then this book will provide you with a guide to filtering out obstacles and enabling implementation focus.

Conventions

In this book, you will find a number of styles of text that distinguish between different kinds of information. Here are some examples of these styles, and an explanation of their meaning.

New terms and **important words** are shown in bold. Words that you see on the screen, for example in menus or dialog boxes, appear in our text like this: "Clicking the **Next** button moves you to the next screen".

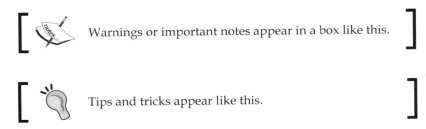

Warnings or important notes appear in a box like this.

Tips and tricks appear like this.

The author has used the following terms to identify specific groups:

- **Customer**: This is used to holistically identify the organization that purchased the software. This would include all Business and Information Technology (IT) organizations.

- **Business**: The specific business organization that is the direct user and benefactor of a business solution. This includes the business owner(s), business analyst(s), business systems analyst(s), and users.

- **IT**: The customer's internal IT organization. This includes functional analysts, technical analysts, developers, and IT strategists.

- **Implementation Partner**: The external Project Services Organization that will provide implementation services to the customer.

Challenge Icon: This icon is used to visibly note a challenge to Customers, Business, IT, and Implementation Partners.

Case Study Icon: This icon is used to visibly note a real world experience with packaged software implementations.

Case Study

Reader feedback

Feedback from our readers is always welcome. Let us know what you think about this book—what you liked or may have disliked. Reader feedback is important for us to develop titles that you really get the most out of.

To send us general feedback, simply drop an email to feedback@packtpub.com, and mention the book title in the subject of your message.

If there is a book that you need and would like to see us publish, please send us a note in the **SUGGEST A TITLE** form on www.packtpub.com or email suggest@packtpub.com.

If there is a topic that you have expertise in and you are interested in either writing or contributing to a book, see our author guide on www.packtpub.com/authors.

Customer support

Now that you are the proud owner of a Packt book, we have a number of things to help you to get the most from your purchase.

Errata

Although we have taken every care to ensure the accuracy of our contents, mistakes do happen. If you find a mistake in one of our books—maybe a mistake in text or code—we would be grateful if you would report this to us. By doing so, you can save other readers from frustration, and help us to improve subsequent versions of this book. If you find any errata, please report them by visiting http://www.packtpub.com/support, selecting your book, clicking on the **let us know** link, and entering the details of your errata. Once your errata are verified, your submission will be accepted and the errata added to any list of existing errata. Any existing errata can be viewed by selecting your title from http://www.packtpub.com/support.

Piracy

Piracy of copyright material on the Internet is an ongoing problem across all media. At Packt, we take the protection of our copyright and licenses very seriously. If you come across any illegal copies of our works in any form on the Internet, please provide us with the location address or website name immediately so that we can pursue a remedy.

Please contact us at `copyright@packtpub.com` with a link to the suspected pirated material.

We appreciate your help in protecting our authors, and our ability to bring you valuable content.

Questions

You can contact us at `questions@packtpub.com` if you are having a problem with any aspect of the book, and we will do our best to address it.

1

The Silo Approach is Alive and Well

For the past fifteen years, I have been what you call a "hands-on" student of the packaged software industry—specifically, Enterprise Resource Planning (ERP) software. One of the hard-learned lessons of early packaged software implementations is that we should not take a functional silo approach to implementing an integrated business solution. Enterprise solutions support business processes, and business processes typically span multiple functional areas (silos). Having a functional silo perspective typically results in underestimating integration considerations. ERP, or any packaged software, is only as strong as its integration across the functional areas that support a business process. As an industry, I can see that we are maturing to take a more holistic approach to packaged software implementations. However, there is room to grow.

Consider the following: business software providers are evolving their applications to be more business process centric. There has also been a resurgence in the subject of business process re-engineering and business process management. "Focus on your business processes!" is the advice that you will hear from analysts and implementation partners alike. Too bad that this advice focuses on only one component of a business solution.

Why do we need to change?

Based upon a survey of customers who have implemented ERP solutions, the overwhelming message is that customers are not satisfied with the business results. The following surveys provide statistical data on the rate of failure of ERP implementations:

- Robbins-Gioia Survey
- Conference Board Survey

Robbins-Gioia Survey

Robbins-Gioia, LLC, a provider of management consulting services located in Alexandria, Virginia, conducted a study of the perception by customers of their ERP implementations. The study included 232 survey respondents, spanning multiple industries, including Government, Information Technology (IT), Communications, Financial, Utilities, and Healthcare. A total of 36% of the companies surveyed had, or were in the process of, implementing an ERP system.

Key findings:

- 51% viewed their ERP implementation as unsuccessful.
- 46% of the participants noted that while their organization had an ERP system in place, or was implementing a system, they did not feel their organization understood how to use the system to improve the way they conducted business.
- 56% of survey respondents noted that their organization had a program management office (PMO) in place, and of these respondents, only 36% felt that their ERP implementation was unsuccessful.

Conference Board Survey

This survey interviewed executives at 117 companies that attempted ERP implementations.

Key Findings:

- 34% were very "satisfied"
- 58% were "somewhat satisfied"
- 8 % were unhappy with what they got
- 40% of the ERP projects failed to achieve their business case within one year of going live

- The companies that did achieve benefits said that the achievement took on average six months longer than expected
- Implementation costs were underestimated for the year following implementation by an average of 20%
- Support costs were underestimated for the year following the ERP implementation by an average of 20%

Nearly 90 % of ERP implementations are late or over budget [1] and the ERP implementation success rate is only about 33%. What are the causes for such dismal results? I am firmly convinced that our expectations and approaches to ERP or any Commercial Off The Shelf (COTS) software implementations are the primary drivers. I will spend some time on a few of the key areas that we need to address in order to improve upon the packaged software implementation experience. First and foremost, what I am talking about is the implementation of a business solution.

Business solution defined

Today, the majority of business software vendors say that they provide business solutions. The term "business solution" is one of the key buzz words used to try to uniquely identify a software product offering. And as such, it is being misused and basically getting "watered down"—just like the term "business process".

I believe in the term "business solution"; however, no software can provide you with a "business solution"—only the vehicle to get your organization from point A to B. Before we can implement a business solution, we must first understand what a business solution is. I like to view a business solution as three components:

- People
- Processes (business processes)
- Technology (software and technical infrastructure)

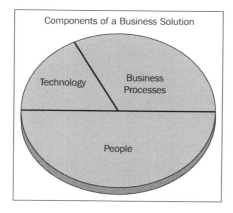

Components of a Business Solution

What is the most important component of a business solution?

Now, here is something interesting to consider: "Do you need all three components to have a solution for your business?" Let me address this in another way, "Do you need software in order to conduct business?" I am persuaded to say that the answer is no. Business was being conducted before the invention of the computer. However, I am quite aware that not having software as a part of your business is not practical in today's competitive marketplace. I do want to demonstrate that software only supports, and therefore can only have a certain level of benefit to, a business. Packaged software does not have the capability to make key business decisions. It is key business decisions that drive business results. Business software can provide information and data to assist people in making business key decisions. Seen in this light, one can conclude that people are the most important component of a business solution. Case in point: I have been on successful business solution implementations in spite of software limitations. I have been on successful implementations in spite of not having all of the business processes clearly defined. However, in my fifteen years of implementation experience I have never been on a successful implementation where the people (i.e., organization) were not ready for the new business solution. People have the greatest impact on the success of a business solution. Is it not interesting to note that the majority of packaged software implementations focus mostly on products and technology.

What is wrong with existing packaged software implementations?

I have listed the components of the business solution in the order of priority and significance. Very often, you will see business solution implementations deal mostly with products and technology during the first three-quarters of the implementation and only at the ending phase of the implementation is there any consideration of the other components of the business solution. Software and technology are important; however, your implementation strategy should not fixate on a single silo. The optimal implementation strategy will focus proportionally on each component of the business solution based upon the impact that each respective area (technology, business process, and people) will have on the implementation's success. To accomplish this change in our implementation strategy, we must first address a couple of popular perceptions in our industry today.

IT does not matter? Think again!

I would like to take the opportunity to note that I do not prescribe to the "IT Doesn't Matter" crowd. It's like saying "I can travel San Francisco to New York without any mechanical means". This is a true statement but how realistic is it in today's competitive landscape? Conversely, the IT community should continue to evolve their support approach where IT supports a business solution—not only software. Software by itself generates no business value. What software can do is enable efficiencies of people in order to produce business results. There is a healthy and optimal balance between the three components of a business solution that is required to generate maximum business value. Each customer and implementation partner must work together to find this balance. One thing is for certain: as part of your implementation, you must focus on all three components in parallel.

Is technology changing Business?

I do not believe that technology is changing business, but rather that technology is finally catching up with leading business practices. For example, back in the early nineties, I read a book on the e-business revolution. The major premise of the book was that technology was transforming existing business models into an e-business model. The book provided an example where inventory stocks could now be checked in retailer stores and inventory orders could be generated to maintain a desired stock level. The book explained that this is an emerging requirement due to new e-business technology.

I have to humbly disagree with this analysis. The above requirement had always been a desire of business. I remember back in the 1950's when my father would make the rounds as a salesman to his retailer customers to see their inventory levels and manually created orders to maintain the retailer's inventory levels. Many businesses did not perform this process because (a) it was manually-intensive work, and (b) it reduced focus on higher-priority business activities. Technology is now providing a cost-effective vehicle to accomplish this business requirement. Everyone has heard the phrase "build it and they will come". This philosophy may have worked out in the era of "green screens" and emerging client/server technologies, but not in today's world. Technology driving the business is like—forgive the cliché—putting the cart before the horse.

It is important to understand and appreciate what technology can and cannot do for a customer. Often, the true problem lies not with the COTS software itself (granted, there are always software bugs and fixes) but rather the demand for quick fixes and rapid cures to the challenges posed by the underlying business model. If the packaged software did not improve the performance of the underlying business model, then executive management would conclude that the implementation was a failure. This statement leads us to the first principle of implementing a business solution:

> *Focus on Business Results!*

Ten principles for implementing a business solution

Following are the ten guiding principles I have developed and utilized in my fifteen years of implementation experience for packaged software:

1. Focus on business results
2. Customers — make an investment in your implementation partners
3. Implementation partners — enable your customers to lead during the implementation
4. Perform business solution modeling
5. Determine the correct implementation approach for your unique business solution
6. Implement to the current business process maturity level
7. Maximize enhancements and minimize customizations
8. Negotiate for success
9. Have a business solution architect role on the implementation team
10. Accelerate decision making by generating more knowledge and less information

Principle #1 for implementing a business solution

Focus on business results

I remember working on my first ERP implementation (in 1994) for a customer where we were implementing a solution for human resources, benefits, and payroll. I was the functional lead consultant for the payroll application. The customer's payroll manager and I were discussing how confident we were with the payroll capabilities of the new ERP system, before the go-live event. I said that I was confident that the payroll process would be handled correctly within the ERP solution but I was unsure about the payroll expense accounting entries generation (which was going to be handled by an in-house utility). Therefore, the payroll manager said we have a payroll issue. I reiterated that the ERP payroll solution is complete and that we could create paychecks. The customer's payroll manager said "I don't care if this ERP payroll system creates paychecks in thirteen different colors! We have a broken payroll process because we cannot complete the final payroll activity: booking to the general ledger!" I must admit I was pretty "wet behind the ears" at the time and this customer's statement stuck with me throughout my career. Customers do not care how wonderful and streamlined the intermediate steps are if the process cannot produce the desired business results! The majority of business results that a customer is interested in are not even produced inside the software itself. For example, running a report is not a business result. A business analyst making a decision based upon information in a report—now that is a business result (the decision).

If the desired business results are not produced, then the implementation will be considered a failure by the customer—regardless of whether the business software was moved into production successfully.

Principle #2 for implementing a business solution

Customers — make an investment in your implementation partner

Customers — one of the key factors that will have a huge impact on your implementation's success or failure is your implementation partner. On average, an implementation of packaged business software costs at least three to six times the cost of the COTS software. This fact is resulting in customers spending more time selecting the best implementation partner possible. However, this should not be the extent of the customer's investment with the implementation partner. Every customer I've worked with has insisted that their implementation was unique — and this is a correct statement!

Revisiting our definition of a business solution, it has been my experience that every implementation is unique in the following areas:

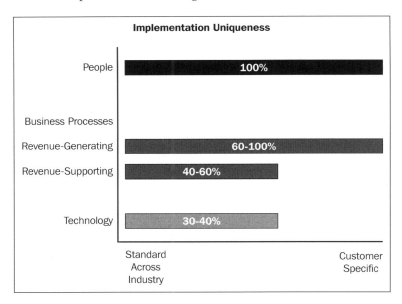

No implementation partner will have a complete appreciation of the customer's business solution until the customer makes the investment to perform knowledge transfer with the implementation partner. The greater understanding and appreciation that your implementation partner has of the customer's existing business solution, the greater the probability of the success of the customer's implementation partner and the enterprise solution implementation.

Principle #3 for implementing a business solution

Implementation partners — enable your customers to lead the implementation

I am an avid hiker. I love to hike and I try to find ways to coax my family to hike with me. I remember the first time that we went on a long family hike, which my wife lovingly refers to as a "death march". I was in the lead, setting the pace. It was a good pace for me but it was difficult for my wife and daughter. You see, my wife and daughter do not hike as much as I do. Needless to say, their experience was unpleasant and it was some time before my wife and daughter would go on another hike.

I suspect that many customers have similar experiences with their initial packaged software implementation. In most cases, the implementation partner was in the lead and most likely had several packaged software implementations under his or her belt. For many customers, the implementation of packaged software was new ground for them. Given the pace, most customers only had time to focus on execution and not on truly appreciating the purpose or objective of their actions. It was a "death march" mentality that resulted in poor customer ownership and user experience. Customers had such a bad experience that afterwards it was extremely difficult to get the customers to upgrade their existing packaged software. Upgrades are a key method to extend the investment and generate additional business value from packaged software. Without periodic upgrades to existing packaged software, the customer will eventually experience a negative Return on Investment (ROI).

I decided to take a different approach on our next family hike. I decided to let my wife and daughter lead the way and I would be in the back, supporting. To my surprise, we made it up the mountain and we enjoyed the trip without losing a substantial amount of time. Even more important was the fact that my family was willing to hike with me again!

The first day of any implementation is the first day of transition from the implementation partner to the customer. Several implementation partners treat transition as the last step in a go-live event. This approach by implementation partners results in a customer not being ready for, or confident in supporting, their business solution. A customer should never feel that way! Allowing the customer to lead will naturally drive the implementation partner to be more focused on knowledge transfer to the customer, which will result in a better success rate for customer preparation.

Principle #4 for implementing a business solution

Perform business solution modeling

For any business solution implementation, gathering business requirements is paramount, and is one of the hardest activities to conduct successfully. And where do you look for business requirements? Business processes, of course. Business processes can be:

- Centralized
- Decentralized
- Country-specific
- Organization-specific
- Customer-specific
- (Even) User-specific

How do you gather these business requirements in a meaningful way that will result in defining a complete business requirements model? How will you identify business requirements that may be in contradiction with one another? How can you validate your business requirements early and provide proof that the proposed business solution will be successful? One of the most important strategies for COTS implementations is maximizing the delivered capabilities of the software. Historically, the majority of packaged software implementation approaches utilize the testing phase as the critical point for solution validation. Unfortunately, this resulted in little or no time to react to unexpected results or circumstances.

Business solution modeling is an approach that will enable you to provide a proof of concept and validation of requirements early in the implementation lifecycle. Business solution modeling delivers hard numbers and results, so that you can quickly demonstrate the validity of the solution. Don't guess what the end result or organization impact will be—prove it! The greatest value that business solution modeling will provide to you is the ability to understand the implications of the decisions that you make as a project team.

Principle #5 for implementing a business solution

Determine the correct implementation approach for your unique business solution

To survive in today's competitive landscape, every implementation partner has their own proprietary implementation methodology. Many customers' internal IT organizations also have their own internal software development methodology. The spectrum of these methodologies range from heavy-weight (i.e., many rules) methodologies like Waterfall to light-weight (i.e., few rules) methodologies like AGILE. For the implementation of a business solution, there are several methodologies involved during the implementation. On top of the software development method is the Project Management Life Cycle that provides guidance on project management activities. If that is not enough, there is Organization Change Management (OCM), Business Process Management (BPM), and Quality Management processes like Six Sigma and Total Quality Management (TQM). All of these processes are relevant and necessary for the implementation of a business solution. How is one to manage all of these different disciplines and build a cohesive implementation approach?

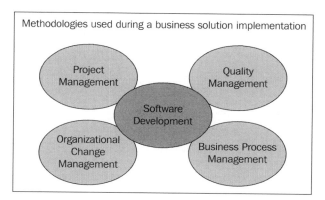

Battle of camps

In the software development camp, there is a relatively new movement and approach (AGILE) that focuses on iterations and embracing change throughout the software development lifecycle. Proponents of the AGILE movement feel that legacy software development and project management lifecycles are too document-intensive, and result in greater cost and less value for the customer. The Project Management Institute (PMI) is considered the authorative source of project management discipline. PMI proponents say that AGILE leads to inconsistent results (not repeatable) and depends greatly upon highly-experienced developers.

Methodologies are not the issue; it's how they are applied that is the issue.

Example: PMI does not stress that a project manager must have some competent level of technical expertise in the area (business) that he/she is managing. In theory, this is in the realm of possibility; however, in today's competitive environment, this can put a project manager at a clear disadvantage. As an exercise in exploration, let us rationally discuss the challenges with having a non-technical expert project manager lead a project. The following represents the assumptions that we are making for this exercise:

1. The project manager is ultimately responsible for delivery of the project. Project scope, cost, and time are the primary responsibilities of the project manager.

2. The project manager is competent in managing projects.

As a project manager responsible for project delivery, and being unfamiliar with the subject matter (technical expert), the opportunity exists for a greater application of project management processes and controls. Until the project manager is comfortable with the approach and the project team, a heavy application of project management techniques will be applied. Recall your first attempt in a new field (e.g., skiing). Were you cautious? Did you take additional steps to ensure success and not failure?

Practically speaking, project managers without the relevant business acumen can control business solution implementation projects, but will have limited opportunities to lead these projects. The market has a way of validating one's conclusions. Specifically, speaking to the ERP implementation market, we are seeing a steady trend in the requirement for project managers to have both software product and industry experience, in order to provide hands-on support and leadership to the project team.

Another example: AGILE, as a software development methodology, is very resource-dependent. A fundamental premise of AGILE is that you have people who are experienced in software development, and experienced at working within teams. AGILE also promotes personal interaction over documents. This can be a challenge when the project team is not co-located, which is becoming more of a reality in this global economy. Would you use the AGILE approach with a team of developers who just graduated from college? The odds are that the answer is no. The point is that there are many factors to consider in selecting the appropriate methodology and determining how to apply the selected discipline.

Soap box—Bashing methodologies

Is there anything wrong with AGILE software development or PMI's project management guiding principles and best practices? No. Both disciples are sound, and have proven track records of success. There are also examples where these methods did not produce the desired results. This does not imply that there are flaws or gaps in either discipline. On the contrary, I have great respect for both groups and their expertise in developing a great source of knowledge that can generate tremendous business value.

Personally, I have a general concern with people who criticize a given discipline without fully understanding the purpose of a specific methodology. Any methodology is based upon a specific environment, which means that you need to have a competent understanding and appreciation of the assumptions, risks, and constraints that a specific methodology inherently has. The project team must conduct an analysis to determine how to apply selected methodologies for a specific project. There is no "cookie-cutter" approach to implementing a business solution.

Customer-specific implementation

Just as an enterprise business solution is specific to a customer, the approach must also be tailored in order to successfully implement the solution. In this book, we will discuss the major implementation approach and provide you (the reader) with insight and variables to consider identifying the "right fit" for your implementation.

In his book on Agile project management, Jim Highsmith makes the following profound statements: "Reliability is results driven. Repeatability is input driven."[2] Too often I feel that we, as implementation partners, focus more on repeatability (driving down price) and less on reliability.

Principle #6 for implementing a business solution

Implement to the customer's current business process maturity level

As discussed earlier, the most important component of a business solution is people. The critical path to any successful business solution implementation is having people prepared and ready to use the new business solution. One of the hardest areas to manage during an implementation is organizational change. A key implementation strategy is to minimize the organizational impact, which will result in a greater probability of success with end-user readiness activities.

The implementation of COTS software will open up new functionality and business activities that the customer may not perform today. Resist the temptation to add new functionality, and only focus on what the customer needs to do today. Limit organizational change, and focus on building a solid foundation. The key to this requirements-gathering approach is to be able to identify the maturity level that the customer is executing within their business process. Capturing and managing requirements to the customer's current maturity level is the accelerated approach for requirements management. Technology alone will not enable a customer to move on to the next business process maturity level. If the organization is not feeling the specific boundary pains of trying to break through to the next business process maturity level, then focus on requirements that will meet the existing business process maturity level. There will be enough organizational change occurring during the implementation. Don't force the technology, or the technology will force you into a corner!

Principle #7 for implementing a business solution

Maximize enhancements and minimize customizations

I consider myself to be a practical person, so I am not under the delusion that packaged software provides for all of the customer's needs and that software changes should not be allowed. I also realize that commercial packaged software will have gaps when compared to the customer's business model, because the marketplace in general drives packaged software requirements, development, and product roadmaps. By default, any software change that you make to packaged software will result in a higher Total Cost of Ownership. The question is: "Is the software change worth the cost?" I like to view software changes in two categories: enhancements and customizations. Enhancements are software changes that result in generating material business value to the customer. Customizations are software changes that result in generating minimal business value. In some situations that I have seen, technology has been used not as an enabler but as a crutch to support customer's non-value added business requirements.

Competitive and transformational requirements are, by their nature, specific to a customer. Enhancements add real business value. Customizations add overhead and complacency. Remember that using packaged software requires a fundamental shift in software expectations. Packaged software makes for an expensive solution! The best practice is to leverage delivered capabilities to their fullest, and focus on software enhancements that generate material value to your business model.

Principle #8 for implementing a business solution

Negotiate for Success

When executive management selects packaged software they are making the following statements:

Building custom software solutions are not strategic to our organization.

However, what is said at the executive level and what is expected among the rank and file can be totally different. Unless you have executive management that can dictate across the breadth and depth of the organization, the project team will have to persuade end users that a complete turn-key solution is not in their best interest. Nothing is free, and this applies to end-user acceptance as well. Negotiating on business requirements is a certainty that must be planned for by the project team. Successful COTS software implementations are those implementations that are able to balance tradeoffs that result in minimizing Total Cost of Ownership while maximizing organizational acceptance.

Principle #9 for implementing a business solution

Have a business solution architect role on the implementation team

If you are asking yourself the question: "Who is a business solution architect?", then this principle is for you. Let's review a business system solution from two different views:

Business Model Perspective	Packaged Software Perspective
Solution	Enterprise
High Level Business Process	Systems
Detailed Business Process	Products
Business Activity	Product Feature Set
Business Task	Product Feature(s)

Typically, implementation partners cover all levels of the software with the following roles:

- Project Manager
- Functional Leads
- Technical Architects

As you make packaged software configuration decisions, you need to evaluate across the five levels of the business model to ensure that a configuration decision does not have an adverse impact on the overall business model. A project manager experienced in a specific business solution will be able to offer insight and guidance at the solution level. Functional leads should have expertise at the product feature level. Technical architects should have expertise regarding the underlying technical foundation that will support the business system.

Who will cover the business process levels? Typically, the implementation partner will leverage the functional lead role to cover the business process levels. Functional leads usually focus on a specific software product. It is important to note that it is very rare to have a single COTS software product supporting an entire business process. Therefore, you need a functional lead that has experience across multiple software products. Many have taken the approach of using traditional project roles to focus on both the products and the business processes, in order to save money. What they fail to realize is that during the implementation the functional leads must eventually focus on the individual software products that they are responsible for configuring. Focusing on business processes cannot be a one time event.

Observations

During my five-year tenure with PeopleSoft's Services Research and Development organization, I had several opportunities to troubleshoot problem implementations of new enterprise-wide packaged business software. A recurring problem with every troubled implementation was that there was not a dedicated functional resource who could focus specifically on the business process and solution level. The business solution architect is a specific implementation role. This role is responsible for understanding how the COTS software supports the entire business process, and provides guidance and validation of software product configurations to ensure that the software configuration will consistently support business activities and objectives across the underlying business model.

Principle #10 for implementing a business solution

Accelerate decision making by generating more knowledge and less information

Making decisions during an implementation is based upon:

- The information available
- Assumption

- Constraints
- The experience of the decision-maker(s)

As an implementation partner, I found myself frustrated many times at the lack of speed with which customers made decisions. However, if I step into the shoes of my customers, I can see that from their perspective they had more assumptions and disjointed data than solid information to make an informed decision. Also, the customer was bearing most of the risk of not making the right decision.

By taking an approach of aggressively gathering information, implementation partners can enable customers to make more timely and accurate decisions. For example, let's visit the PMI PMBOK in the area of cost estimating[3] or what I like to call "levels of understanding". Estimating is based upon our level of understanding regarding effort, scope, assumptions, constraints, and objectives. Generally, for implementations, there are three levels of understanding:

Estimate (Understanding)	Performed Where	Confidence
Order of Magnitude	Scope Initiation	-25% to 75%
Budgeting	Early stages of planning	-10% to 25%
Definitive	End of planning	-5% to 10%

As you move further into the implementation, you are able to better estimate (understand). Question: Why does the confidence range decrease as we move along with an implementation? Answer: We have more proven information on which to base our estimation. Do you think this cause and effect would apply to other areas of an implementation (for example, requirements gathering, testing, or development)? Naturally, would you like to make decisions when you have more information?

For the implementation partners — if you want to enable your customers to make decisions quickly then you need to focus on two areas:

- Aggressively gather information for the key decisions that you know the customer needs to answer
- Present the information in terms that the customer understands, and ensure that the customer appreciates the decision at hand

I use the term, aggressively, because an experienced implementation partner should know up-front the critical-path implementation and configuration decisions that a customer has to make for COTS software. More importantly, the information must be presented in the appropriate manner and at a level that will result in the customer making a decision.

For the customers — we live in a society where we like to keep our options open. Many say that keeping your options open will make you flexible to future opportunities. Many customers have applied this concept to technology and business systems. I have seen this philosophy trickle down into a customer's implementation decision-making patterns. Customers want to have a business solution that is adaptable and flexible. It is totally understandable to require a business solution that is adaptable and flexible. However, customers need to keep two things in mind:

1. Keeping your options open (i.e., not making decisions) will slow down the implementation project and increase your risk of failure.

2. Of all the three components of a business solution (people, business processes, and technology), technology is the least adaptable and flexible. People have the greatest capacity for adaptability and flexibility.

Summary

"Divide and conquer" was a strategy that was ingrained in me during my studies in Computer Science. It is a strategy that I continue to use today to tackle challenges like implementing a business solution. However, what I have learned is that you cannot simply divide a business solution implementation into neat, discrete individual silos, execute in these individual silos, and gather all of the individual results in order to create a successful business solution.

Every business solution implementation is a unique instance that requires research into possible adoption methodologies, as well as how to apply these disciplines during the implementation. The investment strategy that you should invoke in a business solution implementation should be prioritized based upon which areas have the greatest impact on implementation's success. Of the three components of a business solution (people, business processes, and technology), people have the greatest capacity to act, grow, react, learn, and evolve. Investment in your customers, your IT partner, and your Implementation Partners should be the cornerstone of your business solution implementation strategy. Technology and methodologies play a supportive role in successful business solution implementations, yet it is people that have the greatest impact on your success.

A successful business solution generates the desired business results. In the next chapter, we will discuss how to ensure that packaged software implementations focus on value-added business results.

References

1. Martin, M.H., An ERP Strategy, Fortune Magazine, February 1998, Page 95-97.

2. Highsmith, Jim., Agile Project Management, Addison-Wesley, Page 52.

3. Project Management Institute., *A Guide to the Project Management Body of Knowledge*, 2000 Edition, Page 201.

2

Focus on Business Results

Begin with the end in mind. – Stephen Covey

Too often, in packaged software implementations, we readily equate software features with business results. We declare success when software goes into production. We assume (or hope) that the packaged software will drive the desired business results. What we sometimes fail to realize is that software is only one component of a holistic solution that drives business results.

Another slippery slope we deal with during the implementation is the division of labor in order to accomplish project activities. We divide work based upon specialization. This leads to project members having ownership for a piece of the work and limits the project team's ability to validate that the desired business results are achieved. This division of work will also result in additional effort required to organize, direct, and control the work.

The implementation of packaged software is only part of the greater effort of creating a new business solution—an alignment of people, business processes, and technology to support and drive business results. The objective of this chapter is to identify the key techniques that we can employ in order to ensure that every project team member, and thus the project, focuses on the value-added business results.

Challenging today's mindset

Before we can address the limitations of the traditional approach, we must first challenge our current thinking in regard to how we define project objectives, success measures, and scope.

We focus only on what we measure

How can one determine whether the project is focused on business results? I believe that what we measure is a good indicator of what we focus on. Consider the following measurement examples:

- Number of lines of code
- Project budget
- Project schedule
- Number of test defects
- Customer satisfaction

How do these metrics relate to achieving desired business results? I am not inferring that theses metrics are wrong, but what I am saying is that performance-related metrics focused on project execution should not be the only metrics that we utilize.

Project scope fixates on software features

Too often, I have observed packaged software implementations only focus on a subset of a business process, based upon the software features implemented. If you have a project that interacts with a business process then the implementation project needs to examine the entire business process to ensure that the desired business results are achieved. Otherwise, you assume that the upstream and downstream business activities will behave as they did before the packaged software implementation. What is more important to a business—installed software or reliable business results? I am persuaded to conclude that reliable business results are the focus of our customers. Now, let's spend a little time to address the main drivers for business results.

Focus on key drivers for business results

Let's briefly take a look at the key drivers for business results.

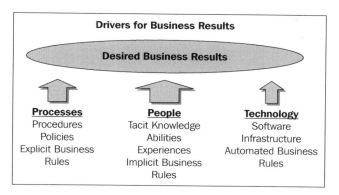

What is important to note here is that the implementation of a business solution not only considers packaged software but also the business processes and people that can have a greater impact on business results.

Technology is a great enabler that can play a role in generating business value. However, technology is not always the right approach to address problems inherent in a business model. Automation of a non-value-added business practice is not generating business value for the customer. "Making decisions and implementing them is where business value is created in an organization."[1] Technology on its own does not have the capacity to consider a diverse range of issues and then act. Knowledge is an attribute of people — not software. Technology can store information, business rules, and other data that can facilitate the decision making process. From a knowledge management perspective, information only generates value for customers when information is applied and a decision is reached. "All of the work that goes into development is not adding value until the software is in the hands of the customer." [2] It is people, not technology, that still make the business decisions that drive results.

Challenge to packaged software providers, and implementation partners

What are the strategic and tactical business decisions that your packaged software can support the customers in making? Leading packaged software providers and implementation partners should be able to provide this information up front to their customers. If the packaged software providers and/or implementation partners cannot provide these decision points then it begs the question of how well the provider/partner understands the underlying business model. If the software provider does not have a competent understanding of the underlying business model then the chances are that there will be significant gaps between the packaged software and your existing business model. Gaps always result in costing the customer money—either as software customizations or business process changes within your organization.

What results generate business value?

Early in my consulting career, I was naïve enough to assume that all business results generated by the customer's existing business model added value. I did not question the requirements defined in the customer's RFPs (Request for Proposals) and quickly proceeded to perform a fit/gap analysis. What I have learned from experience is that there are customer requirements that support non-value-added business activities and results. What I come to understand is that customer required can be based upon both needs and wants.

The traditional approach to requirements gathering and selection is reactive and full of non-value-added effort. The first step is to gather all requirements—regardless of whether a requirement generates real business value. The second step is to categorize and prioritize both the value-add and non-value-add business requirements. The third step is to perform an analysis on whether the packaged software can support the requirement. The final step is to conduct a formal fit/gap session to share the results of the first three steps and determine which requirements will be selected. There are three fundamental challenges with this approach:

1. Wasted effort is spent gathering requirements that support no business value.

2. It is easier to lose focus from the critical requirements that add significant business value. It increases the probability of missing value-added requirements due to a broader approach of capturing business needs and wants.

3. It sets the stage for stressful fit/gap sessions with various stakeholders fighting for their requirements to be selected.

A better approach is to minimize or eliminate non-value-added requirements from being captured up-front. Challenging requirements can be adversarial for IT and implementation partners. It is almost impossible if one does not have a competent understanding of the business model. A practical approach that has worked well for me is to begin with identifying the desirable business results, and then drilling back to the business activities and the corresponding requirements that directly support the result.

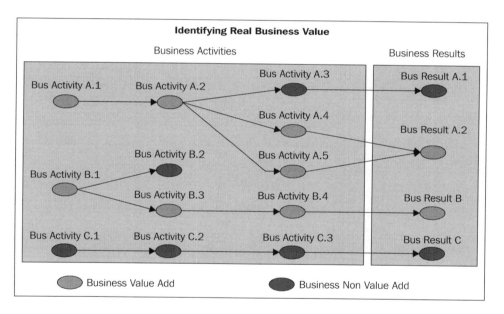

We will use the above illustration to reinforce some concepts. First and foremost is that the customer's existing business model will have both value-added and non-value-added business activities that will drive business results. Also, consider that the existing model may have both desirable and undesirable business results. Performing this type of analysis will take two iterations:

- The first iteration defines all of the business activities and associates these activities with the business results that they support.

- The second iteration focuses on all of the business results and categorizes as value-added or non-value-added. This activity is then performed for the associated business activities.

By conducting this analysis the implementation team can lay the foundation to identify the business requirements that directly support desired business results.

How to focus on business results during an implementation

Now, it is time to turn our attention to practices that we can employ in order to better ensure that the packaged software implementation project focuses on business results.

Conduct business training

An undisputed implementation best practice is for the implementation team to take packaged software product training. I propose that another implementation best practice is for the implementation team to take training on the existing business processes that will be supported by the packaged software.

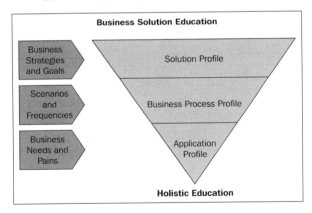

Understanding the business is the responsibility of every individual member on an implementation team. In fact, I would make it a prerequisite! Every individual project role will benefit from the training—including developers, software quality assurance, DBAs, data architects, implementation consultants, and especially project managers. Now, I am not saying that each individual needs to have the same business knowledge as the customer, but there is a basic level of business competency that each member should have. This training will enable a common language to be developed, and will improve collaboration.

Challenge to IT and implementation partners

We should speak in business terms and concepts and not technical jargon when interacting with customers. The responsibility of translation should be on IT and the implementation partners, who should translate technical and software-specific concepts into existing business terminology. This practice improves communication and enables quicker decisions to be extracted from the Business. I understand that the traditional role of a business analyst is to translate between Business and IT — but I fear this is being used more as a crutch and not to encourage every partner to evolve their understanding of the business that they support. There is no better real-time, practical method to align IT with the Business than speaking the language of the Business.

Implementation documentation should be Business-oriented

Data models, generally speaking, end up being not very helpful for understanding the business model. Data models have a limited place and impact. What documentation is more important to your customer — an Entity Relationship Diagram or a Business Process Map? IT and Implementation Partners should have an appreciation for both; however, both parties should strive for the greater understanding on the Business Process Map. Remember that the value of packaged business software is that it should not be necessary to redesign the software. If you have to redesign packaged software then you did not pick the correct software package. Having implementation documentation (forms and templates) geared towards business users will result in encouraging the project team to be business focused.

Use value-added Business results to filter requirements

Let's expand on our previous illustration that identified real business value.

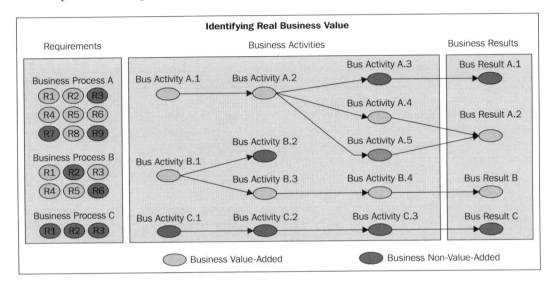

In this illustration, we have business results that are driven by a series of business activities (i.e., business process). Now, we have included a series of business requirements that support the activities for a given business process. The final step of this analysis is to categorize the requirements based upon whether the requirement supports value-added activities or nonvalue-added activities. By focusing on the value-added requirements, we can proactively select requirements and accelerate the requirement-gathering activities. This exercise is not only useful to the implementation partner but also to the Business. It is an approach that can help the implementation team to justify why certain existing business activities are not being carried forward into in the new business solution.

Challenge to customers

Customers always ask what they can do to prepare for their packaged software implementation. Performing a business value analysis on their existing business processes is a key exercise that will help to further refine focus and fit analysis — more so than requirements prioritization. For five years, I supported accelerated implementation approaches and I have concluded that focus is the greatest enabler to rapid implementation.

Project objectives should address business results

Implementing packaged software is not a key business result in and of itself. However, I have observed that the majority of packaged software implementation project objectives are technology oriented. The project objective and scope defines project focus and success criteria. It is key that the project objective clearly address of all the components of a business solution and is business-results oriented. A basic project management principle states that the implementation project objectives and scope should align with the overall executive strategy for a customer.

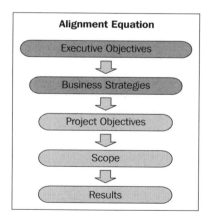

Executive objectives are the highest-level goals for an organization. Business strategies are the high-level approaches to addressing the executive objectives. The project objective and scope are the corresponding tactical efforts required to support the business strategies. The implementation of packaged software is to support business results that satisfy executive objectives. A best implementation practice is to ensure that the project objective and scope can support meeting all of the expected business results by the packaged software implementation.

Summary

Before you can build a business solution, we must first understand the business, and the desired business results that generate real value for the customer. This is the first and most important step in implementing packaged software in such a way that we can provide maximum support to the customer's business value generation stream. Too often, Commercial Off the Shelf (COTS) software implementations focus on the individual functional pieces in silos and fail to validate that the end results — which are typically outside of the business software — generate the business value expected by the customer. Starting with the desired business results and working back to the value-added business activities that the packaged business software should support is an approach that will assist implementation teams in quickly focussing on what is important to the customer.

Alignment is key to being able to produce the desired business results. There are several key alignments that we need to develop and manage as part of the packaged software implementation. First is the alignment between the customer's executives and the project team with regard to project objectives and results. Second is the alignment between Technology (IT, Implementation Partner, Packaged Software Provider) and the Business with regard to the business model and the value-added business results. Third is the organizational alignment between the business model and the packaged software. These alignments cannot be one-time events, but must take place every day during the implementation project. In the next chapter, we will discuss how to effectively create alignment with implementation partners by performing a formal knowledge transfer on the existing business solution.

References

1. Dawson, Ross., *Developing Knowledge-Based Client Relationships*. Butterworth Heinemann, 2000, Page 7.

2. Poppendieck, Mary and Tom., *Lean Software Development: An Agile Toolkit*. Addison-Wesley, 2003, Page 1.

3
Invest in Your Implementation Partners

It's a well known fact that implementation costs have a significant impact on the Total Cost of Ownership for packaged software. Historically, the implementation cost for packaged software averages between four to six times the costs of the software. Given the significant investment in both software and services, many customers have been more aggressive in reducing implementation costs and accelerating Return on Investment (ROI). In my observations, I noted the following approaches to reducing implementation costs:

1. Customers have taken on more responsibilities during the implementation. Typical areas include end-user training, organizational change management, software development, and project management.

2. Implementation partners have provided automated tools to streamline and accelerate certain implementation activities. Typical areas include data conversion and end-user training.

3. Implementation partners are now providing off-shore, or near-shore development options that provide services at a reduced rate.

While these approaches are good, the impact is not as great when compared to the strategic approach of making an investment in your implementation partner. What if I can define an approach that will increase your implementation partner's efficiency by 30 to 40 percent? Interested? Then, please allow me to describe the most effective method of reducing packaged software implementation costs—by conducting formal knowledge transfer with the implementation partner.

Making the investment

To maximize the value and speed of your implementation partner, the customer needs to adopt a common framework that supports effective communication and alignment. Let's take a look at the following illustration:

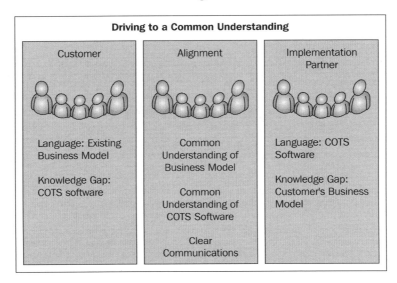

First, we need to understand that the customer and the implementation partner are coming from different perspectives. Both parties have strengths and weaknesses. The customer best understands their existing business model and the underlying success drivers. The implementation partner understands the packaged software and has years of experience in implementing the packaged software. Alignment is achieved only when a common understanding of the business model and the packaged software is shared by both the customer and the implementation partner. When this alignment occurs, there is effective communication and faster decision making. The faster one can make decisions, the faster one can implement. Faster implementation means more effective use of the implementation partner and less costs. Next, we will spend some time defining the activities that the customer can undertake in order to expedite this alignment process.

Document existing business processes

This is an area that I see lacking in many packaged software implementations. For the amount of effort that the customer would have to put into this activity, the benefits are tremendous and far-reaching-from selecting the correct packaged software, to performing a detailed organizational impact analysis during the implementation. I believe that the primary reason why customers do not adequately document their business processes is that no firm direction is given to customers regarding how important this activity is to the implementation.

There are three perspectives to consider when looking at business processes:

- The definition of and relationship of business activities and business rules.
- How the organization executes on the business activities.
- The definition and relationships of business systems (for example, a systems diagram).

Too often, the customer's effort of documenting their business solution model is confined to a system diagram. An optimal approach is to document business processes in a format that marries these three views.

First, a process swim-lane that identifies business activities and relates these to the resources (people and systems) creates a holistic picture of the business solution. Not only will this approach document business process activity, but will also identify how the organization supports the business process. This information will be key when the customer change the business process and identify the organizational change impact, as well as when identifying the segregation of duties. Also, documenting business processes will put your organization in a better position to manage your business processes. You cannot manage what you cannot see! It is also difficult to correctly determine the results from an implementation project if you do not understand your existing business process performance and defined metrics up-front. Effective organizational change management requires that you first understand your current business model.

In the next section, we will discuss a business process documentation approach that I have developed though working with customers to support their packaged software implementations.

Enterprise modeling approach

The primary view of your business process models should be a workflow perspective of the business processes. Key pieces of information to capture in your business process models include:

- Who does what when
- What event triggers the process to begin
- What tasks are performed
- What is the task sequence
- What are the handoffs and dependencies (designation)
- What processes are automated by a system (designation)
- What is the process result

In general, activities should be ordered from top to bottom, and left to right.

By their very nature, business processes can be complex, dynamic across multiple boundaries, and generally a combination of automated and non-automated activities. A common mistake is to assume that business processes for small customers are simple. Usually, it is the opposite due to business execution variability.

Having a documented business model allows the implementation partner to have a holistic view of the customer's business activities and identify knowledge gaps that your customers will have about their business (if your customer does not have existing business processes defined then the odds are that there are knowledge gaps). It's like the saying "We don't know what we don't know". The first step towards business process management is to make processes explicit.[1]

Challenge to customers

Don't be surprised if you experience hesitation and resistance to documenting existing business processes. A typical challenge you will get is "Why spend time building content that will change?" business process models are hard to document because documentation requires effort, but going through the exercise will bring to light key business process decisions that should be made by the customer. Defining business processes can make people fear losing whatever creativity and freedom they have in being able to do their jobs as they see fit. It identifies what is going right and what is going wrong within the business — sometimes independent of the software solution. I have observed this in cases where customers have used packaged software as the driver for addressing existing business process execution issues — which can be a challenge when the problem is caused by a business activity (or lack thereof).

You should address hesitation and resistance by focusing on the value that documented business process models can provide:

1. It creates opportunities to streamline processes and reduce cycle times by identifying non-value-added activities.
2. It supports the comparison of the "As Is" business model to the "To Be" business model, resulting in an exact understanding of the organizational change.

Documenting business processes not only enables the implementation partner to quickly understand the customer's business, but it also puts the customer in a position for identifying additional performance opportunities including:

- Business Process Management
- Lean Six Sigma
- Total Quality Management

Build trust in the implementation partner

Have you ever worked in an environment where you worked in a team where you did not trust the people that you worked with? Did this environment allow the team to be its most productive? In most situations, the results come at a higher price. Trust is the underlying foundation that fosters and promotes the most effective collaboration. There is the old adage "Trust is earned". On the surface, this sounds right, and customers may feel that implementation partners have ultimate responsibility for this. However, customers need to understand that implementation partners will bill the customer in the process of earning their trust. Therefore, it is in the customer's best interest to mutually work together to build the trust that the implementation partners need in order to collaborate effectively.

 Challenge to customers

Customers must be as concerned with building trust with their implementation partners as much as implementation partners are concerned with developing and maturing their relationship with their customers. Developing trust with the implementation partner will foster greater innovation and dynamic interactions which will accelerate implementation activities and reduce costs.

Consider this: as the level of trust decreases, the amount of effort, cost, and cycle time will increase. Why? Implementation partners have a responsible to manage their image to customers. If an implementation partner perceives that they are in a politically sensitive area with their customer, then the implementation partner will naturally perform additional due diligence activities to ensure that their interests are protected. Simply put: the customer will most likely pay more for the additional non-value-added work, and there will be no incentive for the implementation partner to stretch. In my fifteen years of implementation experience, I've never seen a packaged software implementation where the scope of the work was "clearly and exactly" defined. During the implementation, the partners will be asked to stretch. Will they stretch, or will they reallocate resources and cut corners elsewhere in the implementation?

This effect is even more pronounced with fixed price contracts. Yes, the implementation partner is legally responsible for the end deliverable, and the customer will pay the same amount no matter what the effort. Yet let us be practical and reason together. A successful implementation partner is one that can build relationships and make a profit. For a customer to say "Not my problem — you have to absorb the cost" is not indicative of a mutual partnership; it is more indicative of a customer-vendor relationship. Both parties will naturally lean towards doing the least amount of work to maintain the basic relationship. The delivery of product(s) and services will take longer, and the value generated will be significantly less than the value that the customer expects.

The above commentary is not an excuse for implementation partners to not hold their end of the bargain or to create unprofessional leverage. Nor do I blindly subscribe to the statement that "The customer is always right". If the customer is always right and they know what to do then they need to look for cost-effective staff augmentation and not an implementation partner. If a customer is looking for an implementation partner then the lowest level of value that the implementation partner can provide is staff augmentation. If you, the customer, want to harness all of the business value potential from your internal IT organization and implementation partners, then you must make the effort to develop and foster a trusting environment in which innovation is encouraged and not seen only as a risk.

So how can customers build trust with their implementation partners? As I have spent the majority of my career as an implementation partner, I have developed the following suggestions:

1. Treat each member of the implementation partner team as a member of the organization — not an outsider.

2. Be consistent in your expectations and ensure that the implementation partner knows exactly what has been requested and what is not required.

3. Build trust with quick wins. Give the implementation partner opportunities to quickly demonstrate the value that they can provide, sooner rather than later. If there is a misalignment between expectations and results, then it should be addressed early in the implementation.

Educate the implementation partner on the existing business solution

Have you ever been to a seminar or round-table discussion where a group of implementation experts sit on a panel and answers questions from the audience? If you have attended these types of sessions, then you have most likely observed that the information provided was (a) general in nature, and (b) did not generate tremendous value for your company. You had to analyze and internalize the information in order to determine what information was applicable to you. Far too often, this also occurs during a business solution implementation between the customer and the implementation partner. It is not a question of whether customers are sharing information on their existing business environment, but rather how the customer is sharing and presenting the information. Too often, the sharing of information is sporadic, unstructured, and unorganized. Too often, I have heard customers say to implementation partners (including myself) "I've already told you what you need to know. Quit asking me the same questions!" What I would like to address and propose is a new approach to educating the implementation partner that will maximize your information sharing efforts.

Just as the implementation partner should progressively train the customer on the packaged business software package, an iterative approach should be taken by the customer when educating the implementation partner on the existing business model. Education is an iterative process. First we learn, and then we internalize what we learn in order to create understanding. Your implementation partner will not learn and understand the customer's existing business model in one session. The customer's approach must provide the opportunity for the implementation partner to internalize what they have learned before moving to next level of understanding. The levels that the customer should progress through when educating their implementation partner:

Level	Description	Suggested Duration
Business Solution	Provide an executive overview of the existing business processes, systems, and organizations that make up the existing business solution.	4 hours
Business Process	Provide a work flow of a business activities that result from a business event. Key variations and exceptions should be noted.	2 hours for each business process
Business Activities grouped by Role	Provide a "day in the life" experience for key roles that support the business solution.	1 hour for each role

When the customer conducts the current business solution training, it is very important that all members of the project team attend.

Using the approach described above will result in the following:

1. Every member of the project team will have the same understanding and knowledge of the existing business solution. This will result in less confusion and better team collaboration.

2. Effective use of the customer's time in defining the current business environment. This will reduce the risk of customers repeating information to implementation partners.

3. The customer will undoubtedly learn something new about their existing business solution.

4. Gives the customer a "hands-on" training experience. In the majority of packaged software implementations, customers usually take a "train-the-trainer" approach to delivering end user training.

Providing the implementation partner with structured training on the customer's existing business model and solution will enable the implementation partner to provide more relevant information and recommendations. A key piece of information that will enable customers to provide this type of training is documented business processes.

Complete packaged software implementation questionnaires

Competent implementation partners will use several tools to assist their customers with their packaged software implementation. One of these tools is packaged software questionnaires. The purpose of these questionnaires is to gather information on product scope (which packaged software features the customer will utilize) and how existing business activities will align to delivered packaged software functionality.

How many questions have to be answered as part of a packaged software implementation? On average the customer will answer approximately 20 to 40 questions per functional area. The chances are that you may not be able to answer all of the questions without additional investigation. Implementation partners who can provide their customers with the implementation questionnaires before their arrival will provide customers the ability to accelerate implementations and knowledge transfer. Customers can research and answer questions before the implementation partner's arrival. Providing these first responses also gives the implementation partner the ability to start learning before they arrive. With this research and preparation, the customer can allow their implementation partner to spend more time validating responses and asking the next detailed level of questions, instead of waiting for responses.

Conduct project orientation with the implementation partner

Before an implementation partner can generate real business value for the customer, it is important that the customer first spends the time to ensure that there is alignment between the customer and the implementation partner. This process begins during the procurement cycle, but is completed with the implementation partner's team members. Simply assuming that the alignment trickles down from the implementation partner's sales personnel to the delivery personnel is not enough. As a minimum, the following should be reviewed with the entire implementation partner's delivery team:

1. *Product Scope* – Identify the packaged software products and features that are targeted for the implementation. Also, discuss what software products and features are out of scope for the engagement.

2. *Project Scope* – List the implementation activities that the implementation partner is responsible for completing and the implementation activities that the customer is responsible for completing.

3. *Recommendations made during the sales/procurement cycle.* If there were recommendations or advice given to the customer up front, then the implementation partner's delivery team needs to confirm and validate these as part of the implementation. Remember that these recommendations and advice are given up front in the implementation when information may be limited.

Take the time to validate with your implementation partner's delivery team the project's objectives, scope, and strategies. Misalignment will result in communicating mixed signals, generating waste, and fostering mistrust. All of these impacts will cost both you and your implementation partner.

Complete packaged software training before the implementation partner's arrival

Just as it is important for the implementation partner to understand the customer's business model and your language, it is important that the customer have an understanding of the packaged software and its language. Effective communication is a two-party effort. Taking the required packaged software training before the arrival of your implementation partner will enable the customer to more effectively communicate with your implementation partner.

 Challenge to packaged software providers and implementation partners

Customer training is a vital component in enabling the customer to be successful with the packaged software. Packaged software providers should provide training for every packaged software product(s) that they offer. Implementation partners should advise the customer, recommending training classes and the appropriate sequence in which these training classes should be taken.

What to expect from your implementation partner

In the previous sections, we have discussed recommendations to customers that will enable implementation partners to generate additional value. Now, I would like to change direction and speak to packaged software providers and implementation partners regarding what they should do to promote and assist the customer in making this strategic investment in their success.

Predefined business process models

Packaged software providers and implementation partners should provide a complete enterprise business process model to their customers. The best models are a hybrid of conceptual business maps and software process models. In other words, the model should communicate the software components (products and features) that support a specific business activity. The model should also have a standard hierarchy that addresses the enterprise business process at multiple levels, as in the example shows below:

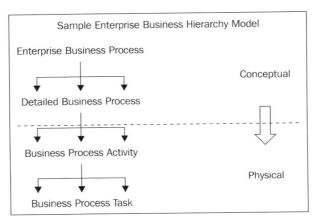

We will now discuss the above exhibit. In our model, we have defined a four-level hierarchy for each enterprise business process. As we move down through our model, to a greater detail, we are moving from a conceptual, or software-independent, view of the business process to a physical, or software-supported, view of the business process. Now, there is a school of thought that prescribes that all business process models should be completely conceptual and independent of software. In this case, you will also need a system diagram that identifies how the software and technology will support the business solutions. To have these models separate is not practical. Typically, what I see is that the business model is scrapped and the system diagram is maintained. Don't get me wrong—system diagrams are great tools for identifying how systems were implemented in the environment, but they are sorely lacking in being able to define what we plan to implement or providing insight into why certain business activities were performed.

Once the enterprise business hierarchy is defined the next definition level should address the detailed business activities performed by the customer.

Detailed Business process maps

The next set of documentation that packaged software providers and implementation partners should provide is detailed business process maps. As a minimum, these maps contain the following types of elements:

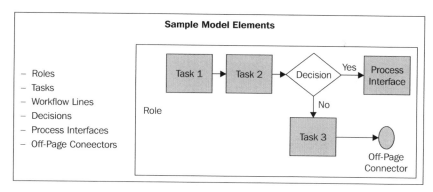

Be careful to note which tasks are automated versus which are manual. Systems, business processes, and people interact together to create a business solution. Now, let's bring it all together and provide an example of a business process map:

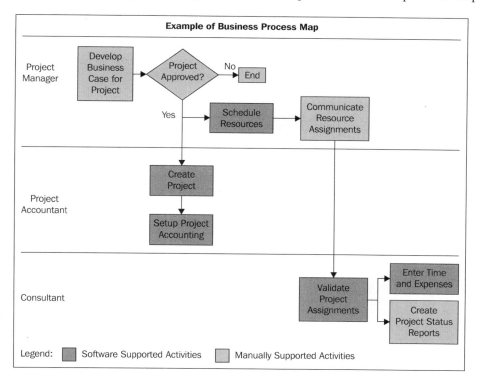

Packaged software providers and implementation partners should provide guidance and examples to assist their customers in documenting their existing business solution. If the customer does not have existing business process maps documented, then I encourage the customer to follow the business process flow documentation standards of the packaged software partner. Using the software provider's standards will facilitate a faster assessment and comparison of the packaged software business model and the customer's business model.

Packaged software implementation questionnaires

The implementation partner should be able to provide the customer with packaged software implementation questionnaires that they can start answering as part of the implementation. These questionnaires should be tailored as much as possible to fit the proposed scope for the implementation. These questionnaires should be provided as soon as possible to enable the customer to start gathering information before the implementation partner arrives.

 Challenge to implementation partners

In the past, implementation partners have been reluctant in providing packaged software implementation questionnaires to customers before an agreement is reached. Implementation partners feel that these questionnaires create a competitive advantage. I also remember when implementation partners stated that having their own implementation methodology created a competitive advantage. Today, every competent implementation partner has their own implementation methodology. What was once competitive advantages are now more of a commodity due to the wide availability of such documents and methods across competitors. Partners are concerned with the success of their partners. Providing implementation questionnaires up front will increase your customer's potential for success.

Certified business solution experts

Methods and tools are only as good as the consultants who use them. Methods and tools provide some level of efficiency and repeatability. However, customers are more concerned with reliability than repeatability. Individual consultants are the greatest source of business value and reliability to customers. Implementation partners understand this and make investments in their consultants to certify their expertise in the packaged software that they are implementing. However, this should only be a first step in the certification process. In addition to software product knowledge, the implementation partner should have certification processes to validate the consultant's industry and implementation knowledge. It is unrealistic (and costly) for a customer to spend weeks educating consultants on a business model. Consultants who only have software product knowledge can only provide staff augmentation support and not the business advisory service that leads customers down the best path for success.

Summary

Every implementation of packaged business software is a unique experience for both the customer and the implementation partner. The implementation partner may be able to draw from similar implementation experiences; however, this alone will not enable the implementation partner to provide the best possible advice and guidance to the customer. Customers should make a disciplined, strategic investment in their implementation partner to foster a trusted, collaborative relationship. Implementation partners should provide the guidance and best practices that will enable customers to maximize the value from their packaged software.

Knowledge transfer is the key value an that implementation partner can provide to customers—more than any staff augmentation services that they could provide. However, it is important to note that any implementation partner cannot provide true knowledge to a customer until the implementation partner has a competent appreciation of the customer's business model. Information about a business solution package that is not framed within the context of the customer's business model is—to be totally honest—just information that the customer has to decipher. To maximize the value that the implementation partner can generate the customer must make an investment in the success of the implementation partner. In a true partnership, your partner's success results in your own success. In the next chapter we will outline a key approach that implementation partners can take to ensure long-term success for their customers.

References

1. Smith, Howard and Fingar, Peter,. *Business Process Management – The Third Wave*. Meghan-Kiffer Press, 2003, Page 77.

4

Enable the Customer to Lead During the Implementation

Knowledge transfer is only the beginning to enablement.

A key value proposition that implementation partners tout is the knowledge transfer that will occur between the implementation partner and the customer (both the business and the internal IT organization). But what is the purpose of knowledge transfer? At the end of the day, what is the result that we are trying to achieve? The only result that counts is having the customer enabled to support and manage their business solution. Now, if knowledge transfer is all that is required to enable the customer to support their business solution, then why don't implementation partners provide operational guides and be on their way? The reason why, is that knowledge transfer is only the first step in a process to enable customers to become self-sufficient with their new business solution.

I think everyone would agree that training (a form of knowledge transfer) with hands-on activities is much more effective than training without hands-on activities. I propose that throughout the implementation, the implementation partner should provide the customer with hands-on experience in the key implementation activities such as business software configuration, and provide them with opportunities to lead in the implementation of the customer's new solution.

Today, many implementation partners handle transfer of ownership as an event or milestone that happens as part of the cut-over to production. We, as implementation partners, too often assume that the traditional and informal "do what I do" approach between consultants and the customer is sufficient for customer enablement. If the traditional approach is sufficient for customer enablement then one can argue that there should be no need for post-production support. When packaged software is implemented in a production environment, it is the first opportunity for the customer to lead in the support of a new business solution. For the majority of customers who do not have hands-on experience with supporting the external packaged software, this can be a difficult challenge. Customers typically ask their implementation partners to provide post-production support until the customer has confidence in the capabilities of their business solution support (technical and business).

Also, consider that the implementation of packaged software is only the beginning for the customer, as they will have to apply software updates, perform upgrades, and implement new packaged software functionality. Too often, customers feel they do not have the knowledge or experience to support all of the packaged software lifecycles, and reach out to implementation partners for guidance. This results in additional cost and effort because the chances are that the customer has to work with a new team of consultants and have to make another investment in helping new consultants understand the customer's unique business solution environment.

I know that there is a better way — an approach that will more effectively provide the knowledge, experience, and capabilities that the customer requires in order to be self-sufficient. Customer enablement will be completed and validated during the implementation. There will be no need for post-production support to address the enablement gap for customers. We will now elaborate on the process that will prepare the customer to lead during the implementation.

Enabling the customer to lead is a process

Enabling the customer to lead is a process that starts with knowledge transfer and ends with the customer proactively taking ownership and leadership. It is not a one-time event but an iterative and incremental process that progressively builds upon the results generated by the previous iteration. Following is the enablement process we will review in the subsequent sections:

1. Educate
2. Enable
3. Empower
4. Celebrate

Educate

Before an implementation partner can conduct effective knowledge transfer with the customer, the customer must first obtain a certain level of understanding and competency regarding the COTS (packaged) software. This is why education is important, and is the first step in this process. As described earlier, another key benefit of formal education on packaged software is that it enables more effective collaboration between the customer and the implementation partner.

However, what I do see lacking in today's packaged software implementation approaches is education on the implementation process itself. To reiterate, customers do not have a wealth of experience when it comes to implementing packaged software. How can we expect the customer to lead if they do not have a firm understanding of what is required to implement and maintain the packaged software? Also, note that implementation training is not just for the customer's business owners, but also the customer's internal IT organization that is partnering in the implementation. As many have learned the hard way, there are several fundamental differences in the approach taken to implement "design from scratch" software versus packaged software. Remember, every project team member must be on the same level playing field in order for effective collaboration and knowledge sharing to take place. Training on both the packaged software product and the implementation process are required to holistically educate the customer.

Best Practice: Knowledge transfer plan

How do you know when a customer has been effectively trained and a complete knowledge transfer has occurred that will enable the customer to be successful with the new packaged software? Revisiting our illustration of a business solution:

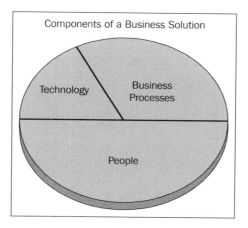

In previous chapters, we have referred to this view and also identified people as the component with the largest impact on a successful business solution. A key enabler for people to be successful is effective knowledge transfer with the implementation partner. For a process so important, it demands that we formalize this process to ensure completeness. For many packaged software implementations, knowledge transfer is a process that is loosely managed and typically results in the implementation partner providing support long after the go-live date.

A knowledge transfer plan first defines the knowledge transfer process and the methods that will be used to conduct knowledge transfer. Second, it defines all of the customer's roles and responsibilities that are required to support the entire business solution— from both a functional and technical perspective. Third, the knowledge transfer plan should act as a checklist for each individual role to validate that effective knowledge transfer has taken place. Following is an example of a knowledge transfer plan:

Knowledge Transfer Plan				
Role	**Description**	**Business Tasks supported by COTS software**	**Knowledge Transfer Method(s)**	**Knowledge Transfer Complete**
Project Accountant	Responsible for creating and managing the project accounting structure and rules for a project.	• Establish project accounting structure • Creating project accounting transactions • Executing project costing reports	• COTs software training (product-level) • Mentoring • Business Solution Overview	Yes
Project Manager	Creates and executes project work plans and revises as appropriate to meet changing needs and requirements.	• Create project requests • Approve project transactions • Manage project work plans	• Mentoring • Business Solution Overview	No
COTS System Administrator	Responsible for the configuration, implementation, and maintenance of COTS software.	• Create software instances • Install updates and fixes • Maintain production job sequences	• Classroom training • Business Solution Overview • Application management training	Yes

Effective knowledge transfer is more than just training and requires a holistic approach, using several methods (training, mentoring, knowledge generation, and interactions) to be successful. The end result of knowledge transfer is enabling the customer to support their new business solution.

Enable

Now that we have laid the foundation with the customer through education, the next step is to help customers internalize their training into the knowledge that they require in order to take more of a leadership role during the implementation. The two leadership styles that implementation partners should use are coaching and mentoring. It is easy to get the concepts intertwined and give the impression that coaching and mentoring are the same. They are not; and for effective knowledge transfer, there is a prescribed sequence. First, we coach the customer then we mentor the customer.

I explain to my customers that coaching is completing their packaged software education. Most customers would agree that one learns much more about packaged software during the implementation cycle than just receiving formal training. This statement is not to discourage customers from formal packaged software training, nor to comment negatively on formal training provided by any packaged software provider. It is a reality that is rooted in the simple concept that education is an iterative process It is a key value proposition for an implementation partner. The customer's implementation partner will complete the customer's packaged software education. Therefore, it is important that a customer selects an implementation partner who can effectively train them. Select an implementation partner who does not have a competency in education, and the customer will have an implementation partner who will struggle to perform effective knowledge transfer.

Coaching is all about teaching and directing the customer. It has been my experience that most implementation approaches focus on coaching as the primary means of knowledge transfer and never drill deeper to encourage the customer to "take the reins" in the earlier stages of an implementation. Here is where mentoring comes in to play.

Mentoring focuses more on sharing experiences and partnering together on implementation activities. Traditional mentoring approaches that I have observed are more around the "do what I do" model. Mentoring has to be deeper than that. Mentoring involves explaining why we do certain implementation activities in a certain order, as well giving the customers the first opportunities to lead and, in some cases, fall. Effective mentoring is motivating, and supporting others to lead.

Empower

I am a huge fan of demonstrating that a desired end result can be achieved. As an implementation partner, I encourage my customers to demonstrate that they understood and internalized what I shared by having the customer lead in the configuration of the packaged software. If my customers are able to configure their packaged software, then I, as the implementation partner, have been successful in enabling the customer to lead and manage their business solution. I follow a simple rule: the more interaction (i.e., hands-on experience) the customer has with the packaged software, the more prepared they will be.

Empowering the customer is an incremental process, and should not be a one-time event. As the customer incrementally demonstrates capability, the implementation partner should incrementally put the customer in the position to lead. For example, implementation partners should configure at most 20% of the packaged business software, with the customer completing the majority of the configuration work with the implementation partner in a supporting role. Sometimes, we, as implementation partners, get a little impatient and jump in to do the work quickly without realizing the disservice that we are doing to the customer. I have been guilty of this mindset in the past. Yet nothing gives me greater satisfaction than when the customer is able to lead during the implementation. It's a time to celebrate and learn.

Celebrate

Customers, have you ever had an implementation partner come to you and say "Congratulations, you have mastered the configuration and support for a certain business process in the packaged software. You now have the ability to support sixty percent of your business software!" Now, don't take this to mean that a celebration is required every time the customer learns something new. However, since knowledge transfer is so important to enablement, it should be tracked and monitored. A good implementation partner will take the extra effort to ensure that their customer is ready and able to independently support their new business solution.

Celebration also provides a learning opportunity — to understand what enablement activities worked, and to determine areas for improvement. This insight will be useful to the implementation partner as they can focus on the next customer enablement knowledge domain. Lastly, celebration builds project momentum. Referring back to the components of a business solution (People, Processes, Technology), people have the greatest capacity to execute and grow during the implementation. Show me a motivated project team and I'll show you a project team that can implement a successful business solution regardless of the limitations of the packaged software.

Enablement requires different leadership styles

A key competency for any implementation partner is their ability to enable the customer to support and manage the new packaged software. This will require the implementation partner to employ different leadership styles during the implementation. There should be a logical progression in leadership styles that naturally transfers ownership from the implementation partner to the customer. We will use the following illustration for our discussion:

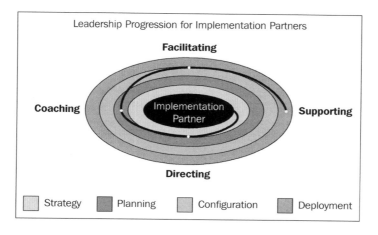

Let's discuss each leadership trait in more detail, in the context of an implementation lifecycle.

1. In the early strategy and planning stages of an implementation, the implementation partner should use a **directive** leadership style to lead the customer. The implementation partner leads in setting the direction and the pace of the implementation.

2. As the customer is educated on the packaged software and implementation approach, the implementation partner moves towards a **coaching** leadership style that enables the customer to take a more active leadership role in the packaged software implementation.

3. With the **facilitating** leadership style, the implementation partner has moved from an active leadership role to a passive leadership role. The customer is leading and managing the implementation project.

4. The **supporting** leadership style is the final stage where the implementation partner provides what I'll call ad-hoc/as needed support and guidance.

Case Study

Let me provide you with a real world example. I was assigned to play the role of a project manager leading the implementation of packaged business software for a Fortune 100 company. The customer had a project manager who I was paired with to manage the project. The customer's project manager did not have any experience with implementing packaged software. Early in the implementation, I took a directive approach in leading the implementation. I used the enablement process defined earlier (educate, enable, empower, celebrate) to transfer ownership to the customer's project manager. As the customer's project manager demonstrated that true enablement had taken place, I changed my leadership style from directive to supportive. At the end of the design phase, I was more of a project administrator assisting the customer's project manager. I followed the four leadership styles described above to enable the customer's project manager to lead during the implementation.

As the norm, the customer's budget was getting tight and they were looking for opportunities to reallocate existing funding to support an important downstream role (functional consultants for software configuration). I informed the customer that I was playing a supportive role and that the customer should reallocate funds to the functional consultants. This was a viable option because I took the approach of enabling the customer to lead during the implementation. I can appreciate that a few of my implementation partner peers may view this as "leaving money on the table", however, if the customer is truly your partner, then this action will only deepen the relationship and result in greater gains to both the implementation partner and the customer in the future.

Implications for implementation partners

Knowledge is power! Knowledge can be money and a key source of competitive advantage for an implementation partner. For an implementation partner, a key concern is balancing knowledge transfer to ensure customer success versus providing too much knowledge transfer resulting in the customer terminating implementation services too early. It's important for customers to keep in mind that knowledge sharing happens more freely in a trusting environment.

In general, there are two types of services that an implementation partner can provide: staff leadership and staff augmentation.

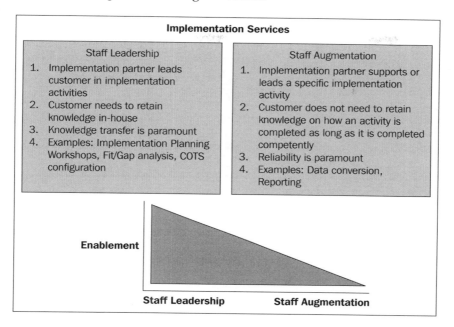

As you move from staff leadership services to staff augmentation services, the level of customer enablement reduces. Staff augmentation is a commodity and does not create a competitive advantage. The core question that every implementation partner must make is whether it will provide commodity services — services that compete on cost and price, or differentiating services — services that compete based upon the customer enablement generated. Staff leadership services have a greater impact on establishing profitable long-term customer relationships. To achieve greater customer enablement, implementation partners should play more of a staff leadership role during the implementation.

Challenge to implementation partners

Implementation partners should formalize their enablement process for customers to a reliable process with specific milestones. Every consultant into the project team should be measured against how well they have enabled the customer to be self-sufficient with the packaged software.

Challenge to customers

The enablement approach defined in this chapter is based upon having a customer who sees their implementation partner as a true partner and not just stuff augmentation. If customers only require staff augmentation then I suggest that customers get it as cheaply as possible, and don't expect any reliable knowledge transfer to occur. However, if this is the first packaged software implementation for the customer then I would recommend that the customer selects an implementation partner who not only assists your project team but more importantly trains and enables your project team to be successful on their own. That is what a true partner would do. To maximize knowledge transfer, the customer needs to foster a trusted work environment. It's in the customer's best interest.

Summary

There are several key reasons for having the customer lead during the implementation. "In general, it is more valuable to help clients make decisions for themselves than to go through part of all of the process for them and provide recommendations". [1] Second, the pace that the customer executes is more consistent with the pace at which the organization can manage change. As I learned in my five-year experience with accelerating implementations: there is no value in moving faster than what the customer's organization can handle. Third, customer empowerment is critical to improving decisions and reducing decision-making cycle time. Enabling the customer to lead will inspire confidence and confidence has a direct impact to decision-making. Finally, customer enablement reduces packaged software Total Cost of Ownership (TCO) because the customer will not require outside help every time the customer needs to change the configuration of their packaged software.

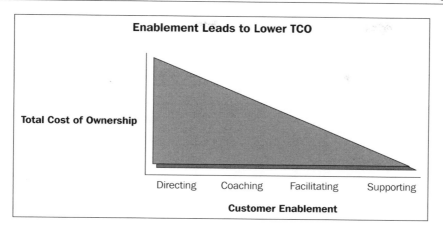

As the customer's ability to support the packaged software increases, the Total Cost of Ownership decreases. When I speak of support for packaged software, I'm not only referring to the technical support required but more importantly the functional support required, including activities like implementing new functionality and adding/updating configuration values.

Today's packaged software implementation approaches talk about the importance of knowledge transfer, but there is really not a lot of content regarding how this is achieved. Knowledge transfer is a key value generator for customers, and implementation partners need a defined process to ensure it happens. Access to structured approaches, when they are useful, is more likely to achieve real knowledge transfer than almost any other single approach. "Nevertheless, it demands a serious time commitment from senior staff, and because the benefits are in the participation, the interaction cannot be reused ".[2] Once you have aligned the project team to the correct focus (business results) and made investments that will have the greatest impact on your packaged software implementation, then we are ready to focus on the implementation methods. In the next chapter, we will discuss a best implementation practice for gathering and validating business requirements for packaged software.

References

1. Dawson, Ross,. *Developing Knowledge-Based Client Relationships.* Butterworth-Heinemann, 2000., Page 96.

2. Dawson, Ross,. *Developing Knowledge-Based Client Relationships.* Butterworth-Heinemann, 2000., Page 134.

5

Perform Business Solution Modeling

Requirements validation is usually too little and too late.

Historically, the majority of packaged business software implementation methodologies are variations on the waterfall software development lifecycle. The waterfall model is a sequential software development process, in which progress is seen as flowing steadily downwards (like a waterfall) through the phases of planning, requirements, design, development, testing, and go-live. One phase is completed before moving on to the next implementation phase.

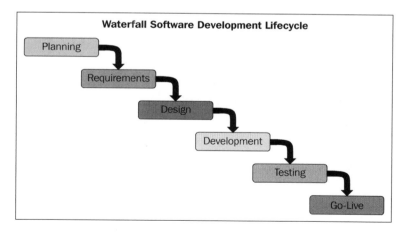

A key challenge when using the waterfall approach is requirements management. Simply stated, requirements management is not only requirements gathering but also requirements validation. Missing a requirement or not understanding a requirement's impact during the **Requirements** phase can be a costly mistake because validation is not completed until the end of the implementation cycle (**Testing**). This late finding will result in additional rework across the **Design** and **Development** phases. Even worse, it may encourage ad-hoc resolution, which creates the opportunity for greater implementation risk and negative impact. What is required is an implementation approach that addresses both requirements gathering and requirements validation early in the implementation.

To further elaborate on the challenges faced, following are the techniques that are typically employed in validating requirements as part of a waterfall methodology:

Validation Technique	Challenge
Peer Reviews	Only as good as the peer's experience with the business software and knowledge of customer's business model.
Customer Reviews	Makes the assumption that the customer understands every activity and variation of their existing business model.
Testing	Happens late in the implementation cycle with not much time to address issues or unforeseen circumstances.

The disadvantages of the waterfall model arise from the difficulty of fully specifying requirements at the beginning of the project, before any design work has been done and before any code has been written."[1]

Another challenge that is typically overlooked is reconciling conflicting requirements. The implementation team need to understand which requirements are in conflict before you can address them. Unfortunately, in the quest to reduce implementation timeframes, I have observed that requirements for packaged software are gathered in parallel across functional business areas. This increases the risk of gathering requirements in isolation, which increases the likelihood of conflicting requirements. Fit Gap sessions may be able to identify conflicting requirements.

Fit Gap sessions are sessions where business requirements are compared against the delivered packaged software functionality to identify requirements that can be supported by the packaged software (Fits), and identify requirements that cannot be supported by the packaged software (Gaps).

Depending on how the Fit Gap sessions are conducted, the implementation team may have the opportunity to identify these issues—however, the odds are against the customer because Fit Gap sessions will not naturally identify requirement conflicts. If you have an experienced and knowledgeable implementation partner, then they may be able to proactively identify conflicts based upon their previous implementation experience.

How can we address these challenges inherent in a traditional waterfall implementation approach? First, we need to realize that effective requirements management should be an iterative process. In the fifteen years I've spent participating in and monitoring system implementations, I have never seen a case where all of the requirements are defined and validated in one session or event. For such a critical and strategic step in any business solution implementation, does it not make sense to take an iterative, risk-adverse approach for defining requirements? Prototyping and business solution modeling are two activities that complement one another in enabling the project team to define and validate business requirements.

Defining prototyping and business solution modeling

Today, in implementation discussions, we hear the terms *prototyping* and *modeling* used interchangeably to describe *experimentation*. However, I believe that these are separate activities with different objectives, and should be performed at different points of time within a packaged software implementation. Both prototyping and business solution modeling support key requirements management activities.

Requirements management consists of three key activities:

1. Requirements gathering
2. Requirements analysis
3. Requirements validation

Prototyping focuses on facilitating requirements gathering, and business solution modeling focuses on requirements validation and impact analysis. We will discuss both of these activities in greater detail.

Prototyping

Prototyping is a useful form of experimentation for facilitating the gathering of requirements—especially when business requirements are unknown or evolving. Prototyping also provides the foundation to start requirements gathering. Prototyping is a recommended activity when business need(s), the mission-critical requirements, or the implementation approach for the business solution has not been defined or agreed upon. Prototyping typically focuses on one component of a business solution—software. It is hard to focus on all three components of a business solution when you have so many unknowns in the software component. As you evolve the "unknowns" into "knowns" within the software component, this will facilitate decision-making in the other components (processes, people) of the business solution.

Prototyping is very useful in the early stages of a COTS/packaged software implementation—even before the start of an implementation project (e.g., software product selection). A best practice for packaged software selection is to conduct prototyping sessions with the packaged software. This activity will provide real-life examples of how well the packaged software fits within the customer's environment. If the customer plans to use an implementation partner, then consider having the implementation partner lead the prototyping sessions. This is a great opportunity for the implementation partner to demonstrate to the customer that they can successfully lead the packaged software implementation.

Prototyping is emerging as a best implementation practice for packaged software. Using packaged software to facilitate requirements gathering actually accelerates requirements gathering and refines evolving requirements. Instead of only using the traditional requirements gathering approach of interviewing and having the customer fill out software product questionnaires, consider leveraging the packaged software itself, via prototyping sessions, to assist in defining requirements.

 Challenge to implementation partners

Implementation partners should consider providing prototyping or "proof of concept" services to their customers that are considering packaged software. These services provide more insight and knowledge than a typical software product demonstration. It is also an excellent opportunity to demonstrate the implementation partner's leadership and the value that their organization can provide to the customer.

Challenge to customers

In addition to the software functionality feature criteria, the customer should define business scenarios and variations that can be incorporated into their business software requirements. The majority of Requests For Information (RFI) or vendor selection criteria focus more on silo functionality rather than the integrated feature sets necessary to support a business process.

Business solution modeling

On the other hand, business solution modeling is less about experimentation and more about validation and the quantification of impacts and results. Modeling is all about getting it right before you move forward to execution. I can understand and appreciate the reality of changing requirements, but we must first understand why the requirement is changing. Is it because the underlying business model has evolved since we undertook this project (and if that is the case, then this should raise a red flag that the project team are spending too much time on experimentation for a point-in-time business solution) or is it because the project team is evolving in their understanding of the business model? Business solution modeling provides a structured approach that enables the project team to move towards a common understanding and develop an appreciation of the underlying business processes.

Business solution modeling is where you start refining your focus on exactly what is required for the implementation. Remember, we are implementing a point-in-time business solution within a specific business process maturity level. At some point during the implementation, the project team has to draw a line in the sand or continue experimenting. Following is an analogy of how prototyping and business modeling play an important role in a packaged software implementation.

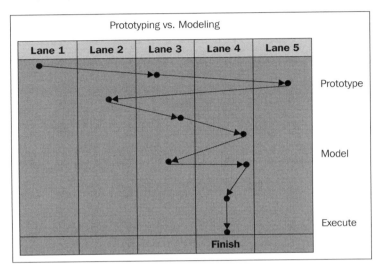

Implementing a business solution is a marathon. There is no one step that will provide the project team with a complete and comprehensive implementation strategy. Every implementation is unique, which means that no implementation partner will be able to give you, the customer, a complete prescriptive approach. Referring back to the above picture, there are multiple options (lanes) available to consider as part of any packaged software implementation. It is important that a process exists to investigate options and generate information for making the correct decisions for a COTS implementation. Prototyping is the first step in performing due-diligence to ensure that every one (Implementation Partner, internal IT organization, Business) agrees on the vision and the approach.

As the project moves from prototyping to business modeling, the main objective is to narrow the implementation focus to a point where it is predictable and the project team can efficiently execute a validated plan. Business modeling provides the project team with a vehicle for driving to the customer's core business requirements. It gets the entire project team to focus on the solution, and provides the opportunity for additional "hands-on" software training. It provides a basis that can be compared to existing business processes in order to identify, validate, and quantify business process changes for the customer.

A key risk associated with an packaged software implementation is underestimating the cultural impact of major process and structure changes due to implementing the packaged software. Business solution modeling addresses this risk by giving you a full view of how your enterprise business solution will affect your entire organization in terms of:

- Products and technology
- Business processes
- People

Now, let us explore how to conduct business solution modeling for a packaged software implementation.

Conducting Business solution modeling

Business solution modeling is a series of working sessions where scenarios are executed against the packaged business software and the underlying business model in order to validate expected results. Business solution modeling should be conducted through a series of iterative and incremental sessions with the entire project team (do not silo individuals on your project team). These sessions focus on the business processes that will be impacted by the implementation. During each session, the project team will define business scenarios to demonstrate or model the various business processes integrated within the new business solution. The project team has the opportunity to see, early in the project, actual numbers and results, rather than just volumes of documents and flowcharts. The project team can also create their own data and set up custom simulation scenarios. "Most users relate better to seeing working screens than to a requirements document, so working software tends to generate better knowledge faster".[2] We will now define the business solution modeling process.

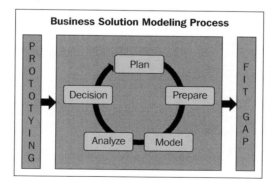

We will describe the business modeling process in the context of an implementation cycle for a packaged software implementation. In the preceding activity, prototyping was conducted to refine evolving business requirements and eliminate configuration options. In business solution modeling, we will conduct one or more iterations of a modeling session in order to better understand and demonstrate how the packaged software will support the defined business requirements. These modeling sessions can also be used to refine or eliminate options for addressing software gaps. After each iteration, there is a decision regarding whether to continue with modeling or move forward with a formal Fit Gap session.

Following is an overview of the business solution modeling process and the key tasks and deliverables for each activity.

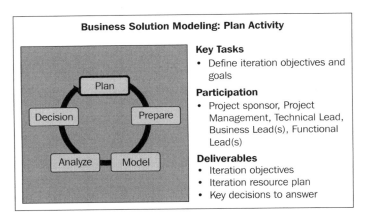

Planning a modeling iteration involves establishing the goals and objectives for each specific iteration. A key discussion to have is identifying the business scenario(s) to model during the iteration. A modeling schedule should be developed to manage the iteration. It is important to remember that the scope of business solution modeling should address all three components of a business solution (people, processes, and technology).

Business Solution Modeling: Prepare Activity

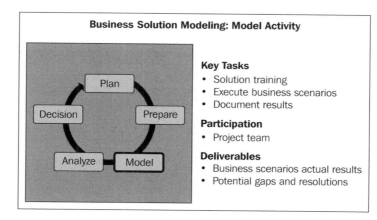

Key Tasks
- Conduct iteration kickoff session
- Define business scenarios scripts
- Prepare modeling environment

Participation
- Project team

Deliverables
- Business scenarios scripts
- Expected results
- Configured modeling environment

Preparing for business solution modeling involves gathering and coordinating the required resources needed to model targeted business scenarios. Conducting an iteration kick-off session will ensure a consistent understanding of objectives, goals, and responsibilities across the project team. Business scenario scripts holistically define business transactions and how the proposed business solution will support these business transactions.

In addition to the business scenario scripts, the project team should also document the expected results. Preparing the modeling environment includes addressing the technical requirements (hardware and software) and data requirements. Required data will include both packaged software configurations as well as the data required to support the business transactions. The required data should be loaded into the modeling environment in order to prepare for the next activity.

Business Solution Modeling: Model Activity

Key Tasks
- Solution training
- Execute business scenarios
- Document results

Participation
- Project team

Deliverables
- Business scenarios actual results
- Potential gaps and resolutions

Solution training enables the project team to see how all the individual components (People, Business Processes, Technology) come together in supporting business results.. The implementation partner should first walk through each targeted business scenario and educate the customer on how the packaged software will support the transaction. This task should include an explanation of data flow, processing, and expected outcomes from the packaged software. No less important, the implementation partner should discuss the organizational roles that will support the business transaction as defined in the packaged software. Once the supporting configuration data is entered into the packaged software, the project team executes testing scripts in order to understand and validate how the software will support the business activities defined in each scenario.

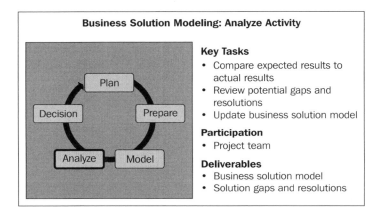

The analyze activity reviews the results from the packaged software. A detailed comparison will be made between the following information:

- Expected results and actual results
- Differences between the current "As-Is" business operating model and the "To-Be" business operating model supported by the packaged software
- Potential gaps and possible resolutions

The last task is to update the proposed business solution definition based on the analysis performed.

Defining the new operational model

A required result of going through business solution modeling is to have a complete, holistic understanding of the components, roles, and interactions that will support the new business model. By having hands-on experience, the project team will have evidence regarding what will work and what will not work.

Creating a new operational model will allow the decision makers to quickly:

- Gain a high level understanding of the new solution
- Identify areas where changes must occur (either of the people, the business processes, or the product/technology)
- Grasp the vision
- Tell the story (A day in the life)

Develop potential solutions to address gaps

As the project team goes through business solution modeling, they will encounter gaps. There are three options for addressing gaps:

1. **Software change**

   Focus on value-added processes that require a software change to the COTS software package. Software changes to support value-added processes can create a material efficiency or competitive advantage specific to a customer.

   Best practice recommendation: Define current business processes as:
   - Strategic, value-added processes that add value to a company's products or services
   - Supporting and Administrative processes
   - Processes that are important to a company's business strategy

   Be ready to work with executive management to prioritize current business processes. Also, look at the lifecycle cost of changing the software. This will assist the project team in determining what options are available for addressing unique requirements. Present the information (full disclosure) in a way that leads your decision makers to arrive at the same conclusion that the project team arrives at to generate ownership.

2. **Business process change**

   If the project team decide to change the business process, then the best implementation practice is to create a business case for the change because (a) if the decision makers do not have all the facts they will not make a decision, and (b) providing a compelling argument can generate user acceptance.

   Not having a complete business case for business process change will increase the risk of requiring multiple fact-finding meetings with the decision makers because the project team do not have all the facts. This will result in less credibility (and more time required) for the project team to gain the stakeholders' acceptance.

3. **Eliminate the requirement**

Keep in mind that automating a non-value-added requirement still will not add value to the business. Customers will have non-value-added requirements that are usually based upon the limitations of their existing environment. The entire project team (Business, IT, Implementation Partners) needs to professionally challenge these requirements in order to determine if the business requirement either (a) creates a competitive advantage, or (b) significantly reduces operational costs.

Revisiting the project charter

Based upon the results from the business solution modeling, the project team should revisit the project charter and determine whether changes are required to the following:

- Scope
- Timeline
- Assumptions and constraints
- Risks
- Deployment strategy
- Objectives

Assess potential organizational acceptance

Based upon the project team's experience with the packaged software during business solution modeling, will the packaged software provide a solution that is acceptable to stakeholders? Can the project team sell this business solution to your organization? What are the areas that the project team can negotiate with key groups in order to gain acceptance? What areas are non-negotiable? To get stakeholders to truly partner, the project team must be able to convince the stakeholders that the new business solution will enable greater value for the organization.

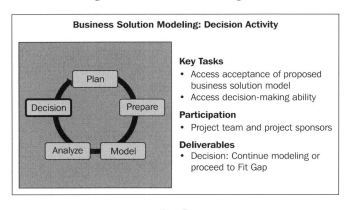

The decision activity determines whether the objectives and goals have been met.

The overall objectives of business solution modeling are to validate business requirements and to identify gaps between business requirements and the delivery of packaged software functionality. The knowledge that the project team gains from business solution modeling will enable accelerated decision making during Fit Gap sessions. An assessment should be made to determine whether the project team can make informed decisions. If there are unknowns, then continue business solution modeling.

To determine whether you need to continue business solution modeling, consider the following questions:

- Have the project team modeled enough business processes and scenarios to feel confident in announcing that the business solution will support the business? It will be the project team's responsibility to sell the solution to executive management and the organization. How can the project team expect to convince others in the validity of the business solution if the team have doubts?

- Does the project team understand how the new operational model will look and fit within the existing organizational structure? Does the project team have an understanding of the organizational changes and technical changes that are required?

- For the critical issues that the project team has defined, do we have enough information to make recommendations to decision makers? The project team must be able to provide the information that the decision makers need to make a decision quickly. Otherwise, it will become a back-and-forth game that may result in your decision makers losing trust in the project team.

Recommendations for conducting Business solution modeling

Following are recommendations I am making based upon my experience in conducting business solution modeling for my customers.

Customer's knowledge of existing business activities

It is vital that the business users participating in the business modeling sessions have a solid understanding of their existing business model—especially when it comes to variations in business processes. However, it is not practical to bring in every business expert to speak on every unique business scenario that may occur in the business today. It is extremely important for business personnel on the project team to proactively reach out to the individual business experts in order to identify business scenarios and their variations.

Another best practice recommendation is to encourage the customer to document their current business processes and operational model. One of the important steps in business solution modeling is to define the future operational model and compare that to the existing operational model. This comparison allows the project team to quickly identify the areas that the project team should address as part of their organizational change management activities.

Use real customer data during modeling

The most effective way to show how the packaged business software will support your business transactions is by using real data. Think of business modeling as a small-scale parallel test. Identify a representative sample of existing transaction data in the legacy systems and model these transactions though the new packaged software. Only then will the project team have concrete evidence of how your new business software will support your existing business transactions.

Best practice: Number of iterations for business solution modelling

Based upon the fact that the customer is implementing packaged software and that the customer has an experienced implementation partner working with them on the implementation, I would recommend three iterations of business solution modeling:

- **First Iteration**: In the first iteration, the project team should focus on the critical path business scenarios and major exceptions/variations to the critical path business scenarios. The implementation partner is conducting these sessions.

- **Second Iteration**: The second iteration addresses additional business scenarios and variations. The implementation partner and customer are conducting this session together.

- **Third Iteration**: The third iteration validates key software product configuration decisions. The customer is leading this session.

 Red Flag: If after the third iteration the project team needs additional iteration(s) before proceeding to Fit Gap then the project team needs to evaluate why. A key reason why additional iterations may be required is due to not having a competent understanding of the existing business model, or not having a complete set of business process scenarios to model.

Core Business practices—consistency

To effectively utilize the power of COTS software, the following areas must be considered and addressed. Firstly, the customer must agree upon a set of standard core business practices across their business model. This action will facilitate the creation of leading practices for the organization, and will drive the customer towards consistency in business results. Secondly, the enterprise solution configuration should be solutions-oriented, not software-product-oriented. Following is an of configuring an enterprise business solution for the Professional Services Automation (PSA) industry.

A PSA solution should support the relationship between Human Resources, Operations, and Sales. In the underlying business model, Human Resources is responsible for providing the necessary resources for Sales (proposals) to position and Operations (service delivery) to use in delivering professional services. Sales and Operations typically use the concept of project roles to identify appropriate resources for service delivery. Human Resources typically uses the concept of job codes to identify responsibilities and qualifications of individuals. To ensure effective Human Resource hiring practices, there should be a relationship between project roles and job codes. Having a relationship between project roles and job codes will promote clear resource expectations across functional boundaries.

Configuration of packaged business software may involve bridging different perspectives of similar information. Having a clear and consistent definition of shared information will promote greater collaboration and integration across the business model.

Have multiple disciplines represented

Implementing a business solution involves multiple disciplines and requires having multiple perspectives represented during meetings in order to ensure holistic discussions. Include Development, Quality Assurance, Business, Project Management, and Business Solution Architecture in all modeling sessions. Each participant must play an active role and bring a unique perspective during the business solution modeling sessions.

Recommended Roles

- **Scribe**
  - Minutes and action items

- **Business**
  - Validating and communicating business scenarios

- **Development**
  - Valid design options and technologies

- **Organizational**
  - Job roles impacted

- **Project Management**
  - Scope management, risks

- **Quality**
  - Business scenarios and variations

- **Internal Controls**
  - Data integrity

- **Business Solution**
  - Requirements Conflicts

Every individual should be gathering information to support their downstream deliverables.

Each member should be gathering tacit knowledge that will enable them and their team to be successful and reduce non-value-added discussions.

 ## Challenge to implementation partners and IT

In this ever growing global economy, we need to become more than software and technology experts. We need to become more than vendors and staff augmentation. We need to become advisors—business solution advisors. We need to continue to evolve and help our business partners and customers correctly apply technology. We need to challenge (in a caring manner) our customers on their software requirements and really ask if technology is the answer! But here is the crux of the matter, if we do not understand the customer's business then how can we challenge or lead? Without a competent understanding of our customer's business, we are, at the end of the day, vendors and not partners. Vendors can be replaced—partners are usually kept for a longer term.

Value proposition for Business solution modeling

This section outlines are the key benefits of conducting business modeling.

Provides a working proof of concept

Use business solution modeling as a demonstration to executive management, business owners, and strategic users that can promote and generate user acceptance earlier in the implementation lifecycle. Be able to provide to executive management and business owners with hard evidence (results) of how the new enterprise business solution will support their organization.

Business solution modeling provides a working model that the project team can present to, and that can help you to appropriately set the expectations of, these groups, instead of having gossip and hearsay set the expectations. Remember that any COTS implementation will be a highly-visible project and must produce visible results quickly. "The longer a team, large or small, goes without delivering an integrated product to a review process, the greater the potential for failure."[3]

Validates software configuration

Generally speaking, packaged software utilizes two types of data: transactional data and control data. Control data defines the packaged software configuration and business rules required to support the product's features. It is important that the project team have an opportunity to evaluate the key control data set-up and decisions before committing to a specific configuration approach. Business solution modeling provides the project team with the opportunity to see first-hand how your configuration decisions will support the overall business model—not just a specific product feature. This validation of the software configuration is especially important when multiple business software products are part of the implementation scope.[3]

Creates a baseline model for impact analysis

With business solution modeling, the project team can see your business processes in their entirety early in the project and can identify, validate, and quantify business process changes. It also gives the project team a baseline model for validating the impact of changing or better-defined requirements at the solution, business process, software, and organizational levels. Having a working software model increases feedback. A key advantage of going with packaged business software is that the project team should have working software immediately available.

Challenge to packaged software providers and implementation partners

If your packaged software provider or implementation partner cannot provide the customer with a working version of the packaged software in the early stages of the implementation, then I would reconsider the partnership. Not have a working version of the business software for prototyping and modeling activities will greatly increase the implementation risk without a potential increase in reward (i.e., it is what the Project Management Institute would define as "pure" risk).

Enables business solution training

Business solution training is an area I see missing in packaged business software implementation approaches. The majority of available packaged software training focuses on individual COTS software products. Rarely is the training focused on how the packaged software supports the complete business process. The challenge is that the majority of these software products support multiple business process threads, leaving the customer to try and piece together an integrated picture. Conducting business solution modeling gives the project team the opportunity to learn how the packaged software will support the business processes. Interweaving software, business processes, and operational role execution into a complete holistic picture will enable the project team to define a "common ground" for effective collaboration.

Identifies challenges early

It is hard to effectively plan if the project team do not know what you are up against. Challenges can not only be software-related, but also business process and people-related. I will also be pragmatic and state that there will always be some software defects in packaged business software (COTS software providers are only human. Really!). Running business scenarios through the packaged software in a modeling environment will enable the project team to proactively identify issues. Identifying defects early will provide the project team with the opportunity to partner with your packaged software provider in defining a solution. Identifying defects late in the implementation cycle will only facilitate a support exercise (a customer-vendor relationship). Partnership will provide the customer with the opportunity to have more influence with your packaged business software provider.

Facilitates and promotes customer interaction and quick decision-making

Business solution modeling allows the customer to be much more involved in the overall design of the business solution, giving the implementation partner and customer's internal IT organization the input necessary to ensure that the solution meets the customer's requirements. Getting customers (strategic decision makers) to make firm decisions may prove difficult when these decisions are only based upon flowcharts and design documents. Generating results from your packaged software will provide the evidence that customers need to make decisions quickly.

Challenges with business solution modeling

As with any implementation approach, there are advantages and disadvantages in business solution modeling. A main drawback is that it is very hard to predict at the outset of the project how many iterations there will be until the project team has a competent requirements model that has been validated. Project planning and the coordination of modeling activities will be an intense process. Also note that we can come to a point in execution where iterations can have diminishing returns. Consider the following illustration:

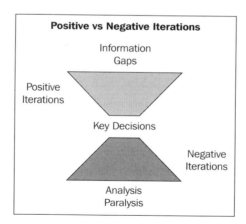

The above diagram shows an iterative approach to generating the information required to make the key decisions required to implement a business solution. It would be ideal to develop all of the information that we need in one single event. However, this approach is not practical. As we continue to perform iterations in generating information, we better understand what we need to do. Also note that each additional iteration refines its focus (reducing the options to investigate), resulting in generating more specific information required to make an **informed** decision. Another take-away from the above illustration is that if no decisions are made then iterations (at some point) can have a negative impact to your implementation.

Signs of negative iterations:

- *Options are not eliminated.* The implementation team cannot keep their eyes on multiple options and continue moving forward. People cannot be infinite for the duration of a project or they will burn out. People need focus.

- *No decisions are made.* Action items can be completed but *decisions* move the implementation forward.

- *No new information is generated.* If an iteration does not generate any information then there is no way for the project team to generate knowledge to make decisions. Either we are losing focus when executing iterations or we are scratching the bottom of the barrel (a very casual way of saying that we may be running up against the law of diminishing returns).

Won't Business solution modelling slow me down? Is it worth the cost?

In 1987, Barry Boehm wrote, "Finding and fixing a software problem after delivery costs 100 times more than finding and fixing the problem in early design phases". In his book on rapid development, Steve McConnell makes the following observations;

> *"If you can prevent defects or detect and remove them early, you can realize a significant schedule benefit. Studies have found that reworking defective requirements, design, and code typically consumes 40 to 50 percent of the total cost of software development (Jones, 1986b; Boehm 1987a). As a rule of thumb, every hour you spend on defect prevention will reduce your repair time 3 to 10 hours (Jones 1994). In the worst case, reworking a software requirements problem once the software is in operation typically costs 50 to 200 times what it would take to rework the problem in the requirements stage (Boehm and Papaccio 1988)"* [4]

I grant one that business solution modeling will add time to your project work plan, but given the potential savings downstream I believe that you would agree that business solution modeling is worth the investment. In fact, I have seen business solution modeling actually reduce the implementation cycle because the iterative modeling sessions enabled customers to make decisions quicker as well as brought discussions to a conclusion. The alternative is to keep dragging them forward to be revisited again and again.

Summary

Requirements management is a strategic activity in any business solution implementation. For an activity so critical to the success of the implementation, it is wise to take a risk-adverse approach to increase your probability of success. A method that is both iterative and incremental will enable your project team to define and validate business requirements in a logical manner. Successful business solution implementations incorporate prototyping and business solution modeling early in the project, so that functional users can iteratively define and test critical business processes prior to formal testing and go-live activities.

Business solution modeling will allow the project team to provide hard evidence to executive management and business owners that the new enterprise business solution will support their existing business. Business modeling will also allow the business process re-engineering team to have an area to work through the changes in the business process flow. It will give change agents an idea of the tangible interactions that a user will have with the new enterprise solution. Simply put, business solution modeling can help the project team take the guesswork out of the implementation. In the next chapter, we will discuss how to select and apply the relevant disciplines in supporting the customer's unique implementation.

Reference

1. McConnell, Steve., *Rapid Development*. Microsoft Press, 1996, Page 137.
3. Highsmith, Jim,. *Agile Project Management*. Addison-Wesley, 2004, Page 250.
4. McConnell, Steve., *Rapid Development*. Microsoft Press, 1996, Page 71.
2. Poppendieck, Tom & Mary,. *Lean Software Development*. Addison Wesley, 2003, Page 20.

6
Determining the Correct Implementation Approach

When Methodologies and People Go Wrong

Webster's defines a methodology as a body of methods, rules, and postulates employed by a discipline; a particular procedure or set of procedures. A methodology can provide tremendous value to a packaged software implementation by providing a process to guide the project team through the implementation cycle. However, it is important to remember that we are implementing more than just software. The end result of our efforts is the implementation of a new business solution. And getting the desired result requires multiple disciples and guiding methodologies to be utilized.

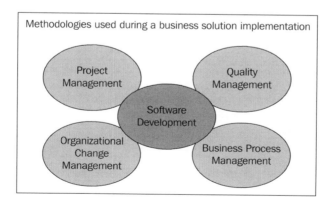

Methodologies used during a business solution implementation

Project Management • Quality Management • Software Development • Organizational Change Management • Business Process Management

Each of these disciplines is vital in effectively supporting a business solution. Each of these areas has emerged as separate discipline in the marketplace for a reason. Too often, I have watched project teams try to utilize a single methodology to address all of the disciplines listed above.

While a methodology provides a proven approach, it cannot ensure that the methodology will be properly used. Following are the common mistakes I've observed with using methodologies during a business solution implementation:

1. Using a single methodology for all disciplines.

2. Executing methodologies in silos or as separate projects.

3. Ignoring the inherent advantages and challenges associated with a given methodology.

I have observed in the marketplace that there is no lack of information regarding the definition of methodologies; however, there is a very small set of information regarding how to 'right-size' and integrate these methodologies to work both efficiently and effectively for an organization that is planning on implementing a new business solution. Therefore, I will attempt to define the key factors that we need to consider in selecting and applying a methodology to a project. In the following sections, we will conduct a cursory review of the leading methodologies, in order to reinforce the principles defined above.

Who is the leader—Business or IT?

A question I see most customers struggling with is "Who should lead the business solution implementation—Business or IT?" I feel that selecting an extreme—either business or IT—is wrong for the following reasons:

- IT will never have a full appreciation of the business model. At the end of the day, it will be Business that will define success.

- Business will never have a full appreciation of the capabilities and limitations of the technology and how to apply it correctly to a business problem. It is not in the strategic interest of Business to be at a level to incorporate detailed IT capabilities within its organization.

Both parties have different drivers. Business is responsible for conducting a special set of business activities, and the execution should support the overall corporate objectives. IT is responsible for supporting individual business technology requirements, as well as being responsible for the overall IT assets of the organization. There is a healthy balance between Business and IT. In the following sections, we will address this balance as it relates to business solution implementations.

But before we discuss methodologies and project leadership, we must first have a governing implementation approach—a guiding principle/strategy that will ensure that we make decisions in the correct context. Our guiding principle must be a solution-based implementation strategy.

Solution-based approach

A solution-based implementation strategy takes a holistic approach, addressing all three components of a business solution:

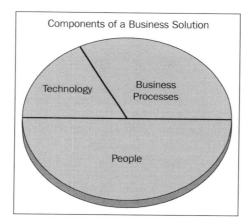

The correct implementation approach will manage all components of a business solution in unison—not in silos. Packaged software implementations must be implemented in the context of a complete business solution. Products and technology alone do not make a business solution; everyone knows this truth all too well. The implementation approach must address all of the components of a business solution (people, business processes, and products) and spend the appropriate level of effort based upon the influence each component has in making the solution successful.

Business solution component: People

People are the single most important factor that will determine whether a business solution is a success or a failure. People can be the most challenging component to deal with in a business solution. Let's be honest, we can program software to do exactly what we want; people are a different story. However, people have the potential of generating the greatest value in the context of a business solution. Finally, people are the most flexible and adaptable component of a business solution. All of these factors should be considered when making a decision of whether to make a Packaged software enhancement or change to a business process.

Business solution component: Business processes

What is a business process? I have seen many definitions but I like the definition provided by Howard Smith and Peter Fingar in their book "Business Process Management — the third wave".

> *A business process is the complete and dynamically coordinated set of collaborated and transactional activities that deliver value to customers.* [1]

We will examine at the some of the characteristics of business processes that are highlighted in the above definition:

- Complete: there is a beginning and an end to a business process
- Dynamic: responding to changing customer demands and market conditions
- Result-Oriented: value is generated for the customer

These basic characteristics must be addressed during business solution implementations, in terms of needs assessment, requirements management, and the validation (testing) of a business solution.

Just as important as addressing the basic characteristics, a business solution implementation must also address the basic components of a business process.

Business solution component: Technology

Software and technology encompasses the technical infrastructure, networking resources, and COTS/packaged software that will support the business solution. With COTS software, there are inherent advantages and disadvantages (challenges), as listed in the following diagram:

Implementing COTS Software

Advantages	Challenges
• Drives standardization across the enterprise resulting in greater operational efficiencies • Enables greater focus on strategic activities • Potential for rapid deployment of technology • Shared IT development costs • Simplifies the IT technical footprint	• Organizational change impact • Perception of setbacks • Discipline to maximize COTS software investment • Different implementation approach (solution driven vs. requirements driven)

In the context of a business solution, it is important to note the following:

- Business leads, and technology supports
- Technology is the least flexible component of a business solution

It is vital to develop an implementation strategy that maximizes the advantages and minimizes the challenges associated with COTS software. As a project manager, I've displayed the above slide at the beginning of every working session (Requirements Gathering, Design, Fit Gap) to encourage the project team to make decisions that maximize their COTS investment. The business solution based approach will be the guiding principles that the project team will use as they address the different disciplines required to implement a business solution. Now we will spend a few moments defining these disciplines.

Disciplines used in a Business solution implementation

In any business solution implementation, the following methodologies (disciplines) are critical to solution success:

1. Project management

2. Software development

3. Organizational change management

4. Business process management

5. Quality management

We will now briefly define each of these disciplines. The objective of this discussion is to provide a backdrop for the recommendations being made in the remainder of this chapter.

Project management

As defined in PMI's Project Management Body of Knowledge (PMBOK), project management is the application of knowledge, skills, tools, and techniques to project activities to meet the project requirements. PMI provides a comprehensive process, which includes the following project management activities:

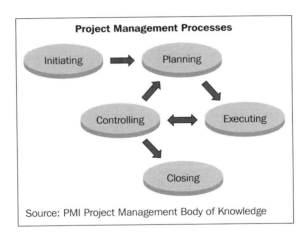

The PMI's PMBOK defines a standard project management method that can be utilized across all project types (implementation, construction, and so on). Although all of the processes (initiating, planning, executing, controlling, closing) are present in every type and size of project, the degree of execution can vary greatly based upon the project type and size.

Now that we have completed our brief definition of project management, let's move on to the next discipline, software development.

Software development

Software development (engineering) is the application of a systematic, disciplined, quantifiable approach to the development, operation, and maintenance of software, and the study of these approaches; that is, the application of engineering to software.

There are several software development methodologies to choose from in order to create the implementation approach for the business solution. The best practice is to find the software development methodology that best fits with your organization. A key analysis to perform when choosing a software development methodology for a project is identifying the advantages, challenges, and assumptions associated with each methodology. The following is a high-level analysis of the most familiar and common software development methodologies. This is not intended to be a detailed analysis but more of a cursory review in order to reinforce the principles outlined in this chapter.

Methodology	Advantages	Challenges & Assumptions
Waterfall	• Useful for well-defined software products	• Document-intensive • Few visible signs of progress • Late validation of business requirements
Code-and-Fix	• Easy to learn • Supports a rapid approach	• No assessment or validation of business requirements • People-dependent (only a very senior developer can make this work) • Not a repeatable process
Spiral	• Risk-oriented • Quick visible signs of progress	• Additional project coordination and project team discipline is required • No definitive stopping point • Increased risk of requirements conflict in downstream iterations

Methodology	Advantages	Challenges & Assumptions
Design to Schedule	• Shows software in successive stages (iterative) • Guarantees a production-ready software after a certain stage	• Planning requirements are high • Unnecessary planning and requirements management work performed if the project does not get to all stages before go-live
Evolutionary Delivery	• Useful for soliciting emerging requirements	• Increased risk of requirements conflict in downstream iterations
Design to Tools	• Supports a rapid approach	• Lose control over software direction
Crystal Family (Agile)	• Supports a rapid approach • Personal interactions over documentation	• People-dependent (experienced software development and business) • Will be a challenge for project teams that are not co-located
Rational Unified Process	• Iterative process • Component-based (use case)	• People-dependent (experienced software development and business) • Increased risk of requirements conflict in downstream iterations

This is only a brief analysis of the software development methods available today. What's important here is to illustrate that every methodology is based upon a set of rules and assumptions. A project team needs to consider how well their implementation can adhere to a method's rules and assumptions.

Hybrid implementation approach

What if there is a way to take the key advantages from existing software development methodologies and combine into an implementation approach that is both risk adverse and accelerated. An implementation approach that is flexible enough to support emerging requirements and yet quickly confirm stable business requirements.

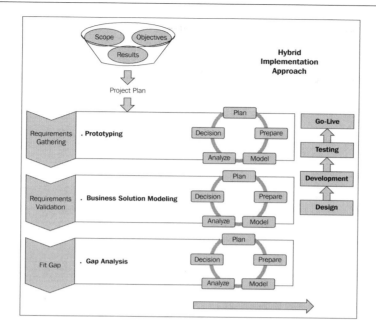

In general, the perceived areas of risk in an implementation lifecycle should be managed with an iterative, risk-adverse method. With a packaged software implementation, the typical area of greatest risk lies in requirements management. There are three key activities performed in requirements management:

1. Requirements Gathering
2. Requirements Validation
3. Fit/Gap

As defined in the illustration above, an iterative approach should be taken to ensure that all relevant business requirements are defined and validated. The additional investment the project team makes using an iterative approach will accelerate the downstream implementation phases. A comprehensive requirements management approach addresses both software requirements and organizational requirements. We will now focus on the discipline that is typically underestimated in business solution implementations: organizational change management.

Organizational change management

Organizational change management is the process of deliberately influencing the human and organizational aspects associated with a project, in order to achieve the desired results. Organizational change management deals with the coordinated development of business processes and worker skills. Based upon an analysis of the popular organizational change management methods out in the market today, the following are the key activities for a business solution implementation:

Organizational Change Management

Mobilize	Define	Plan	Execute	Validate
Align executive management sponsorship	Current Business Model	Organizational Change Management Plan	Communicate	Adoption
	Future Business Model		Field Readiness	Enablement
	Assess Organizational Change Readiness	Communication Plan	Deploy	
		Field Readiness Plan		
	Strategic Change Agents			
	Organizational Requirements			

The above overview is not meant to show all of the detailed required organizational change management activities, but to focus on the key activities that must be integrated with the other methodologies. In other words, there will be deliverables from the other methodologies that will have an impact on organizational change management activities.

Business process management and Quality management

I decided to address business process management and quality management together because I believe they holistically address the maturity lifecycle for a business process.

Business process management is a systematic approach to improving an organization's business processes. Business process management includes activities to make business processes more efficient, effective, and adapta[ble?] in an ever-changing environment.

Quality management is focused not only on the quality of business result[s], the means to achieve it. Quality management consists of the following processes:

1. Customer focus
2. Quality planning
3. Process management
4. Process improvement

At one time, I thought that Business process management and Quality management were competing methodologies, but in studying Lean Six Sigma, I have found that these methods complement one another in a logical progression. This logical progression is best defined in the Lean Six Sigma DMAIC process.

Business Process Management				
Define	**Measure**	**Analyze**	**Improve**	**Control**
• Project Section Tools • PIP Management Process • Value Stream Map • Financial Analysis • Project Charter • Multi-Generational Plan • Stakeholder Analysis • Communication Plan • SIPOC Map • High-Level Process Map • Non-Value-Added Analysis • VOC and Kano Analysis • QFD • FACI and Qual Charts	• Operational Definitions • Data Collection Plan • Pareto Chart • Histogram • Box Plot • Statistical Sampling • Measurement System Analysis • Control Charts • Process Cycle Efficiency • Process Sizing • Process Capability	• Pareto Charts • C and E Matrix • Fishbone Diagrams • Brainstorming • Detailed 'As-Is' Process Maps • Basic Statistical Tools • Constraint Identification • Time Trap Analysis • Non Value-Added Analysis • Hypothesis Testing • Confidence Intervals • FMEA • Simple and Multiple Regression • ANOVA • Queuing Theory • Analytical Batch Sizing	• Brainstorming • Benchmarking • TPM • 5S • Line Balancing • Process Flow Improvement • Replenishment Pull • Sales and Operations Planning • Setup Reduction • Generic Pull • Kaizen • Poka-Yoke • FMEA • Hypothesis Testing • Solution Selection Matrix • 'To-Be' Process Maps • Piloting and Simulation	• Control Charts • Standard Operating Procedures • Training Plan • Communication Plan • Implementation Plan • Visual Process Control • Mistake-Proofing • Process Control Plans • Project Commissioning • Project Replication • Plan-Do-Check-Act cycle

Source: Lean Six Sigma - DMAIC process

We do not plan to discuss each detailed DMAIC activity; however, in the following sections, we will discuss the key activities that the project team should integrate into the overall implementation approach. Now that we have briefly described the relevant disciplines required for a business solution implementation, we will focus on the key factors that the project team needs to consider when selecting the correct methodology.

Selecting the correct methodology

With several methodologies for each discipline to choose from, the question becomes "Which one should I choose?" The following is a list of the key factors that the project team should consider as part of their methodology selection:

Factor: Size of the implementation

What is the size of the packaged software implementation? When considering size, we need to look not only from a financial perspective (cost) but also from an organizational perspective (i.e., users impacted, stakeholders).

Factor: Personnel capabilities

A methodology is only as good as the people using the methodology. It is very important that the people on the project team (Business, IT, Implementation Partner) have the necessary abilities and training to successfully apply a given methodology to a packaged software implementation.

Factor: Risk

What are the risk(s) associated with the packaged software implementation? How risk-tolerant is the customer? Does the customer have prior experience with packaged software implementations? What is the criticality of the solution being developed? If there is a high level of risk associated with the packaged software implementation, then the project team may want to select a methodology that is more risk-averse (iterative).

Factor: Business-IT relationship and culture

The customer should perform a realistic assessment of the relationship between their Business and the internal IT organization. If the relationship does not foster effective collaboration or there is a known alignment challenge, then this presents a significant project risk. An iterative approach should be considered in this situation—especially when it comes to software developments for packaged software enhancements and customizations. "Iterations provide a dramatic increase in feedback over sequential software development, thus providing much broader communication between customers/users, and developers." [5]

Business model dynamics

The more dynamic a business model is, the greater the opportunity for evolving requirements. A dynamic business model requires a method that is rapid and flexible. For example, a revenue-generating business process (Sales) will be more dynamic than a revenue-support business model (Payroll). Traditional approaches, like Waterfall, that focus on a reasonably-stable set of requirements may not be the best choice for this environment.

Factor: Guiding principles for a methodology

As stated earlier, every methodology is based upon a set of rules, definitions, and principles. It is very important that the project team understand the basis for a given methodology as well as determine the assumptions made. Violating the guiding principles will have an adverse affect on the implementation. Making an objective evaluation of the methodology will identify its advantages, challenges, and any assumptions made.

It is important for the project team to perform an assessment of the methodologies available in order to ensure that the correct methods are used, given the customer's environment. Too often, both sides of the aisle (Implementation Partner, IT) use the same old methodologies that they have used for years, without conducting a serious analysis to identify the best approach.

Challenge to implementation partners

s are looking to implementation partners to be thought
terms of recommending the best implementation approach
ed software. As we have highlighted above that the
implementation strategy and approach must change, based upon
the customer's unique environment. Therefore, the implementation
partner needs to be flexible, and competent in multiple
implementation approaches (Waterfall, Iterative, Prototyping,
Agile). There is no "cookie cutter" approach, because each customer's
implementation is unique.

Once the project team has identified the appropriate methods, the next step is to
understand how to apply and integrate the individual disciplines for a business
solution implementation.

Applying methodologies for COTS implementations

The challenge now at hand is how to apply these different methods to a COTS
implementation. The first step is to understand how these disciplines relate to one
another as part of the business solution implementation.

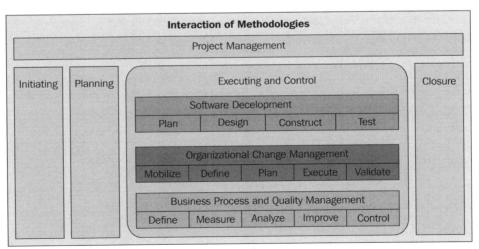

Integrating methodologies

It is important to note that a single methodology cannot provide all of the disciplines required for a business solution implementation. Also, we will find that these different methodologies will have activities in common. The question becomes "How should we integrate these different methodologies together?" Following is a set of guiding principles to assist with integrating these methods:

1. Lead with the method that was developed for a specific domain.

2. When implementation activities are addressed by multiple methods, then select the method that provides the more relevant guidance for packaged software implementations.

Let me provide an example. For the project management domain, I would lead with the project management discipline as prescribed by the Project Management Institute (PMI). However, I know that the project management method defined by PMI is a standard approach across all project types. As a best implementation practice, I would review the project management activities, as defined in the software development method, to refine my project management method and ensure that I have the most relevant approach for the specific business solution implementation.

We will now spend some time looking at each methodology, with regard to leading practices for packaged software implementations.

Project management

I would like to focus on a few key factors, to provide some perspective in applying project management principles for packaged software implementation.

Silo versus holistic focus

In the majority of packaged software implementations performed today, we continue to have functional separation because we do not have the organizational structure and motivational components required to support an on-going holistic focus. Therefore, project management will play a key role in keeping the implementation focus relatively aligned.

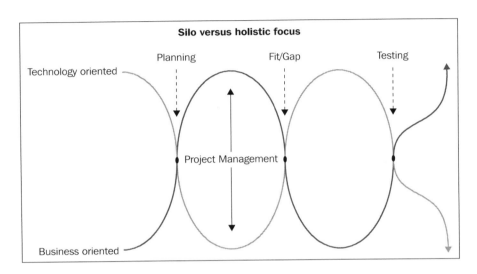

In the illustration above, we can see where the project management approach needs to bridge the gap between a technology-oriented perspective and a business-oriented perspective. The key objective for project managers is to iteratively reduce this gap to a point where both perspectives are in alignment.

Project control

What should we rather control: the (implementation) process, or the end result of an implementation? Which of the two areas is more important to your customer? Some would say that there is not a difference between controlling processes and controlling the end result or the business value, and that by controlling the implementation process you control the business result. I agree that we can indirectly control the implementation result by controlling the implementation process, but is that enough?

The primary driver for determining project management control should be based upon the project resources' capabilities and experiences. Project control can provide only a certain level of business value and therefore should be used prudently. Additional project control will run against the law of diminishing returns. It is important to note that project control is not a substitute for education! Typically, the argument I hear is that project managers do not want to burden the project team resources with additional responsibilities and therefore, project resources receive only a cursory level of information regarding project objectives, scope, constraints, and assumptions. This is not a viable excuse for not educating the entire project team. Everyone is responsible for a successful business solution implementation. The project manager cannot be at all places at all times during the implementation. It is important that every project team member fully understands the project objective, scope, assumption, and constraints in order to proactively govern project-related discussions. The best method to control scope is to address potential scope changes immediately at the source. Project managers need to make an investment in their project team to enable them to become proactive in identifying and addressing potential control issues.

Risk versus reward

Implementing any business solution is a risky business. However, without risk there is no reward. The key is to be able to take smart risks.

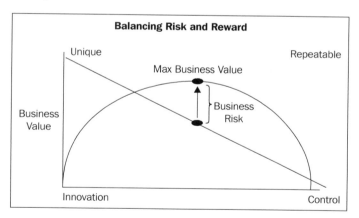

Every COTS implementation is a unique experience. With this unique situation, the project team will have opportunities for innovation. There *must* be some level of innovation for the implementation to be successful. Conversely, there *must* be some level of control in order for the implementation to be successful. As the level of control increases, the level of innovation decreases. Business risk involves the opportunity of generating additional business value. Business is about taking risks. The question is whether it is a smart risk to take.

Balanced project leadership between Business and IT

This last section deals with the specific area of project leadership. For any packaged software implementation, there should be shared leadership between IT and Business:

- Sponsorship: Both IT and Business
- Project management: Both Business and IT
- Project team: For every IT role, there should be a corresponding Business role. Interaction, not documentation will be the major vehicle that will enable each group to better understand and appreciate one another. Knowledge transfer will be most efficient and effective at the interaction level.
- There will be phases within the implementation where naturally you should have a Mentor-Mentee relationship between Business and IT:

  1. Vision or Strategy: Business is the leader
  2. Planning: IT is the leader
  3. Design:
     1. Functional: Business is the leader
     2. Technical: IT is the leader
  4. Construct:
     1. Software: IT is the leader
     2. Operating policies and procedures: Business is the leader
     3. Organizational change management: Business is the leader
     4. Product configuration: Business is the leader

Are we saying that IT should participate in Organizational change management and Business should participate in Technical design reviews? Absolutely! There is no better way for each party to better understand and appreciate each others' core responsibilities. Knowledge often emerges from the collaboration of people with different perspectives on a specific area. Implementation partners should encourage their customer's Business and IT personnels to maximize interactions.

Just as it is wrong to silo applications, it is wrong to silo project team members. Being able to understand and appreciate each other's project roles facilitates more effective collaboration and synergy. I believe that the maximum benefit we get from people is when we broaden their understanding, not specialize it.

Challenge to IT

In their excellent book on Lean Software Development, the authors describe software development as follows: "Software development is a discovery process in which technical people make continual tradeoff decisions in order to reach what they consider an optimal result".[3] Can I challenge you in this area by asking how involved is Business in your software development process? There is no more practical means of removing the so-called "IT-Business" divide them by involving Business in IT-related activities and getting IT involved in the Business-related activities.

Software development

Software development methodologies play a key role in any packaged software implementation. A software development methodology's key value to a packaged software implementation lies in building software enhancements and customizations for packaged software. However, the majority of existing software development methodologies are not a best fit for overall packaged software requirements management, simply because these methods are based upon the principle of building software from the ground up. I understand that this is strong statement, but consider the developments of the EPIC (Evolutionary Process for Integrating COTS-based Systems) software development methodology. This method was developed by the Software Engineering Institute in partnership with Carnegie Mellon University to provide a software development methodology that better leverages packaged software components.

Evolving approaches like EPIC are gaining traction in the marketplace. However, adopting a new software development methodology is not a quick transition and should not be used on large-scale projects until the customer's Business and IT organizations have hands-on experience in using the methodology. Based upon my experience, the majority of IT organizations will utilize their existing Software Development methodologies to support software development activities for packaged software implementations. Therefore, the following sections address how to tailor existing Software Development methodologies to better support packaged software implementations.

Sequential development versus business process development

In general, the majority of software development I've encountered during packaged business software implementation is what I call sequential development. Sequential development focuses on each individual software change (component) separately, then brings the individual components together for a system test. Typically, these software change components are assigned across multiple resources to accelerate development. This development has several inherent risks, including (a) the potential risk of not address conflicting requirements, (b) multiple developers working on related components whose interaction results in an undesirable user experience, (c) not focusing on supporting business value. Remember that a system can only support a business value if the developer(s) can focus holistically to see where business value is supported. Sequential development has the potential to foster disconnect between IT and Business regarding where value generated (misalignment).

On the other hand, business process development starts with the end result in mind. Taking a business process-oriented approach will assist not only with identifying conflicts and ensuring a consistent end user experience, it'll also bring together the concept of executing unit testing and integration testing together.

How is this applied? On a previous implementation, we had a major business process that was supported by two systems. A specific high-level business process-project initiation required customizations in both supporting systems as well as developing an interface. From a business perspective, all of this work is to support one process. It will be viewed and evaluated as one process. Should it not be developed in one process? Yes, we have multiple technical components that will support the business process. However, the development should be done holistically and not in individual components.

Tailoring software development for COTS

Existing IT methodologies are not geared towards implementing COTS software. In general, existing IT methodologies are usually based upon one of the classic software development methods and the primary assumption of said approaches is that you are building the software from scratch. This approach must be adapted for implementing packaged software. Let's take an example of how the approach should change for existing Software Development Life Cycles (SDLC):

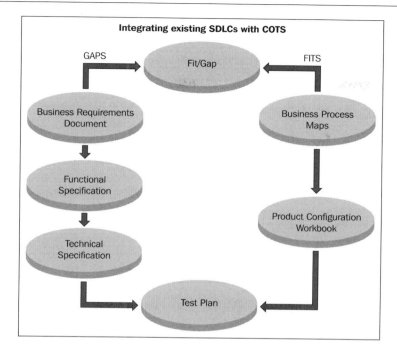

With every COTS implementation, at some point in the implementation, a Fit/Gap is performed. A Fit/Gap session is a comparison between the business requirements and the delivered packaged business software functionality. The key deliverables from a Fit/Gap session are the following:

- List of business requirements that can be satisfied by configuring software product functionality (Fit).
- List of business requirements that cannot be satisfied by configuring software product functionality (Gap).

In general, Gaps are addressed via one of the following options:

- Business process change (adapt to the software)
- Software change

IT methodologies should be used to address software customizations and enhancements. Your implementation partners' implementation methodology should be used to address packaged software configurations that fit the business needs.

Organizational change management

Organizational change management is a key method that will enable the most important component of a business solution to be a success with the new business solution—people.

The success of a packaged software based business solution is much less dependent on selecting the best-of-breed software and more on field readiness and putting customers in a position to capitalize on their investment. Packaged software adoption affects the architecture, business processes, people, and procedures. The challenge I see with existing implementations today is that most implementations treat organizational change as a separate project where there is limited interaction with the packaged software implementation. We will revisit the organizational change management method overview and identify the key touch points with the packaged business software implementation.

Organizational Change Management				
Mobilize	Define	Plan	Execute	Validate
Align executive management sponsorship	***Current Business Model*** ***Future Business Model*** Assess Organizational Change Readiness Strategic Change Agents ***Organizational Requirements***	Organizational Change Management Plan Communication Plan ***Field Readiness Plan***	Communicate ***Field Readiness*** ***Deploy***	Adoption Enablement

Bold - Key touch points with packaged software implementation

Defining the current business model the and future business model

- Defining the current business model supports the knowledge transfer that you need to perform with your implementation partner (see chapter 3: *Invest in Your Implementation Partners*).

- Having the current business model and future business model defined are key components in helping the customer quantify the organizational impact.

 Challenge to customers

Resist the temptation to think that documenting the existing processes and organization is a waste of effort. Bear in mind that identifying and quantifying organizational change requires you to compare the "As Is" business model to the "To Be" business model.

How would you be able to define and quantify organizational change if you have no basis for identifying what is changing? As you document existing processes, keep in mind the end result. The purpose of documenting existing processes is to enable yourself to better define the organization change—not to provide a blueprint for packaged software to replicate.

Organizational requirements

Referring back to the Fit/Gap activities performed during a COTS implementation, we can address gaps either via software or business process change. With gaps addressed via software, you have a functional specification and a technical specification document that will define in detail what needs occur in the software. Should we not have the same level of specificity in business process changes required to the organization? It has been my experience that these sets of requirements are not well defined during the Fit/Gap. In his book on successful COTS implementations, Nick Berg[6] identified organizational requirements as a key nonfunctional requirement that should be identified and documented. These organizational requirements should be addressed as part of the organizational change management plan. Fit/Gap sessions tend to focus only on one component (software) of a business solution. Fit/Gaps sessions should be conducted to address all requirements (software, organizational, technical) for a packaged software implementation.

Field readiness plan

To put it simply, field readiness encompasses all of the activities necessary to prepare and enable the organization to be successful with the new business solution. Organizational field readiness is aligned with the following key packaged software implementation activities:

1. Testing
2. End-user training
3. Production cut-over
4. Support

Traditional implementation approaches spend the majority of their effort around software readiness and limited effort is spent on organizational readiness. In order to experience greater packaged software implementation success we need to reverse this trend.

Deployment strategy

Deployment may not be considered a methodology per se; however, it is a very important strategy that must be considered as part of the overall implementation approach. We can build the perfect business solution, yet fail miserably if the wrong deployment strategy is used. There are two major categories of deployment strategies for packaged software: *Big Bang* and *Phased*.

- *Big Bang*: The new business solution is implemented in its entirety at one time across the entire customer's organization. This includes all of the COTS software functionality defined as being in scope for the implementation, as well as the supporting business process changes, procedures, and organizational readiness.

- *Phased*: A subset of the new business solution is implemented for the customer. The subset (i.e., phase) is typically broken down into the following areas:

    ○ Software-driven: Module/Application/Feature set

    ○ Organization-driven: Location(s), Divisions

    ○ Business-driven: Revenue stream, Line of Business

Advantages and disadvantages of COTS deployment strategies

Following is a summary of the key advantages and disadvantages with the Big Bang and Phased deployment strategies:

COTS Deployment Strategies	
Big Bang	**Phased**
Advantages • Potential for implementing entire solution faster • Minimal throw-away effort (ex. Temporary interfaces) • Single Testing/Patching cycle	Advantages • Quick wins and results • Reduced implementation risk (smaller target) • Learning opportunities during the implementation
Disadvantages • Increased risk due to larger impact (training, end-users) • No learning opportunities • Longer time to show visible results	Disadvantages • Additional throw-away effort (ex. Temporary interfaces) • Potentially longer time for implementing entire solution • Possible regression testing for previous phases

The majority of packaged software implementations use the Big Bang deployment approach, but we are starting to see more Phased deployment approaches due to the increased risk and longer time for results of the Big Bang approach. However, mostly likely, the key driver for Big Bang is the interdependencies of the packaged software. This has more to do with the lack of information regarding these interdependencies/ interfaces than the fact that they exist. If the implementation team does not taken an iterative approach, or perform some type of business solution modeling, then I strongly discourage any one from using a Big Bang approach. In this situation, the risks significantly outweigh the potential advantages.

For Phased deployments, there is greater project management and coordination involved. There is also the potential of building project momentum that will support your negotiation position. Following are recommendations regarding using the three major Phased approaches:

Phased attribute	Recommendation
Software-driven (module/ application or set of features)	Be careful not to focus only on a functional silo but rather focus on a complete business process. Remember that we are implementing a business solution, not just software.
Organization-driven	Select an entity (e.g., Location, Divison) that is representative of the entire customer's organization, in order to maximize learning opportunities.
Business-driven	Focus on the area that generates the greatest business value for the least amount of time and effort.

Deployment strategy should not drive requirements management

Regardless of the deployment method, it is important that you have a holistic approach to requirements management. Having a phased approach to gather requirements will increase potential requirements and software configuration conflicts. These conflicts will result in rework being performed in future deployment phases.

Global considerations

A significant growth area for packaged software functionality is the ability to support global operations. Supporting global business activities has resulted in several variations that must be addressed via the packaged software:

- Business process differences
- Culture and language differences
- Regulatory and statutory differences
- Multi-currency
- Technology (Unicode, formats—e.g., date, name)

Managing global requirements can be a challenge. A recommended approach is to leverage a key advantage of packaged software—consistency in business processes. The first step is to define a logical progression for your global requirements model. For example:

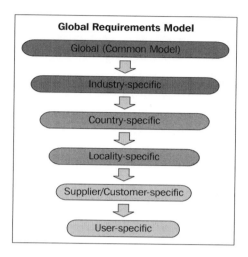

Second, identify the commonalities across the global enterprise in order to create a common set of business requirements that will support a consistent business process. Next, categorize variations to the common set of business requirements based upon more granular categories: Industry, Customer/Supplier, Country, Locality, and User. The goal is to maximize a common set of requirements yet minimize/isolate variations in the core model. This approach will provide the project team with greater options regarding where and how to manage changing business requirements.

Summary

The implementation of packaged business software is always a unique experience that requires the application of multiple disciplines. There are several different methods available to choose from as part of the implementation. After selecting the appropriate methods, the next steps are to (a) understand how each method should integrate with the other methods, and (b) determine to what level you should apply the methodology's principles to your business solution implementation.

Something to keep in mind is that methodologies by themselves do not produce successful implementations. It is people who produce successful implementations. Methodologies provide the strategy and coordination that enable people to focus on producing successful implementations. Now that we have determined the correct implementation approach, the next step is to determine at what level we should support the customer's business model. In the next chapter, we will discuss a best implementation practice for the initial implementation of packaged software.

References

1. Smith, Howard and Fingar Peter., *Business Process Management – The Third Wave*. Meghan-Kiffer Press, 2003, Page 47.

2. McConnell, Steve., *Rapid Development*. Microsoft Press, 1996, Page 240.

3. Poppendieck, Tom and Mary., *Lean Software Development*. Addison-Wesley, 2003, Page. 71.

4. Parnas, David (December 1972). On the Criteria To Be Used in Decomposing Systems into Modules. Communications of the ACM 15 (12): 1053–1058.

5. Poppendieck, Tom and Mary., *Lean Software Development*. Addison-Wesley, 2003, Page 28.

6. Berg, Nick., Secrets to a Successful Commercial Software (COTS) Implementation. iUniverse, 2008, Page 52-53.

7

Implement to the Current Business Maturity Level

The Allure of Technology

Think of the possibilities! Rapid delivery of new functionality! Reduced development cost by quickly deploying prebuilt solutions! If the software does not meet your needs, then use the delivered, user-friendly development tools to customize the COTS/packaged business software. We have the packaged software to make your business more flexible and adaptable.

Most customers do think about the possibilities quickly but have a hard time taking that vision and incorporating it into the realities that are involved in using technology. Both the customer's IT and the Implementation Partner have the opportunity to play an important advisory role to the Business by defining the best approach to take in order to leverage technology when creating a business solution. This advisory role can be a challenge, given the high technology expectations of packaged software.

Features and capabilities

As the story goes, the more features the packaged business software has, the greater the flexibility and adaptability the software has to support your business. Generally, the customer has the option to implement all of the features of packaged software. However, the customer rarely exercises this option, and instead the customer must decide what features to implement. Figuring out which packaged software (COTS) software features to implement can be a time-consuming exercise.

Software design tools

As part of any packaged software demonstration, there is a review and exercise of the delivered software design tools available for customizing the packaged software. In isolation, the process looks simple and straightforward. The objective is to show the possibilities. However, keep in mind the following:

- Demonstrations are conducted by seasoned professionals, typically with both technology and business expertise.
- Demonstrations are based upon sample scenarios in a controlled environment.

Today, there is a plethora of software design tools available for software customizations and enhancements. It looks so simple! However, there is a very simple rule for packaged business software that is often overlooked and underemphasized:

Software changes increase Total Cost of Ownership.

Only when a customer's software change is incorporated into the base code of the packaged software will the software change not result in a reoccurring increase (i.e., upgrades) in Total Cost of Ownership. Upgrade tools can be provided to reduce the impact, but there is still an impact nonetheless.

To customize or not to customize

I have never seen a COTS software package that can provide ALL of the functionality necessary to support all three of the following levels of business solution maturity:

1. Initial (Simple)
2. Best Practice (Efficient)
3. Competitive (Effective)

We have seen strides made by packaged software providers to evolve their product offerings, especially at the Initial and Best Practice maturity levels. However, by their very nature, competitive business processes are unique to a customer and *there will always be a need for packaged software changes.*

When customers ask for my advice regarding packaged software changes, I have the customer focus on the following main points:

- Consider the drivers for purchasing an off-the-shelf software package. What was the business justification for purchasing packaged software? Remember that packaged software targets customers across multiple geographic locations and industries. Two key implied statements that executives make when they select a packaged software solution are (1) having a custom software solution is not strategic to the organization, and (2) we expect our organization to adapt to the packaged software. Strong words I know, however, I have seen a lot of grief and anxiety created during packaged implementations because this message was not clearly articulated to the project team and the organization.

- Is the software change worth the cost?
    - Will the software change result in a *material* reduction in operating cost?
    - Will the software change result in a strategic *competitive* advantage?

- Software changes should never be a substitute for good training. On one hand, there is user-friendliness or efficiency requirements and on the other hand, there is "dummy-proofing".

- Is the software change marketable? Will your customization generate an opportunity for your packaged software partner to reach additional customers? If so, then negotiate with your packaged software provider regarding co-developing the software change. Co-development can be a win-win situation, where part of the development cost is shared, as well as assurance that your software change will be incorporated into the baseline software.

The above advice is not intended to replace the need to perform the appropriate value analysis. Unfortunately, the majority of value analysis performed today is short-term in nature (e.g., ROI) and does not take into consideration the entire software lifecycle impact (development, maintenance, upgrade). When it comes to packaged software, it is important to include the ongoing upgrade and maintenance costs associated with any software change.

Challenge to packaged software providers

Now, let me spend a little time on the other side of the fence. Based upon my experience, I can say that it is not always easy to make software changes to COTS software. There have been improvements made by packaged software providers to provide a more cost-effective method for supporting changes, specifically in the areas of identifying and migrating software changes to future releases. Because there will always be a need for software changes, COTS software providers should continue to provide further support of software changes to their packaged software:

- Upgrade and maintenance tools to identify and transition software changes—especially around automatically identifying impacts of existing software changes.
- Build flexibility into the packaged software where changes are likely:

  1. Business rules/workflow: One of the biggest initial advantages of ERP was the ability to provide data and a non-technical method to get data in the hands of business users; to be able to provide a non-technical, user-friendly method for business users (for example: managers) to tailor their business rules and workflow. Business rules and workflow take a lot of time and to define effort during requirements gathering and fit/gap analysis due to variations across the business. "Business rules, and the ability to change them effectively, are key to improving business adaptability." [1]

  2. Additional user options so that users can create their own unique user experience. This capability can be very useful in fostering user adoption, by enabling the end user to change the look and feel to be more like what they are accustomed to. And these user options should be upgradable to the next software release.

3. Build software features with multiple levels of maturity. I have noted several customizations where capabilities/fields on a page were hidden because the functionality was not being used and the customer wanted to streamline the entry page. Give the customer flexibility to decide which level of maturity is required. As the business process matures, the customer can select the next level of maturity that will result in additional capabilities to become available.

Customers need more than just packaged software savvy implementation partners who gravitate to software as the means to addressing business needs and wants. Implementation partners need to have competent knowledge of the packaged software but more importantly, must understand how to appropriately apply technology and software to a specific business model. Understanding how a business solution matures is the first step in being able to leverage packaged software correctly.

Challenge with technology-driven change

"Build it and they will come", to quote a popular movie. Well, I have learned the hard way that the above approach does not work when it comes to packaged software implementations. There is a simple rule that I keep in mind when I work with customers on their implementations:

Business drives and technology supports.

This simple rule expresses the correct relationship between business and technology. I am seeing more instances where technology alone does not provide a convincing argument for business change. Without a convincing argument, it will be very difficult to foster the user adoption for the technology solution. If user adoption is low, then user error and technology misuse will naturally increase. We can have a technically-competent solution that is not generating the desired business results. Only when Business realizes the pains and limitations of their existing business model, will Business be motivated to adopt the change. For implementation partners, being able to access a customer's business solution maturity level is a method we can use to highlight probable business pains that need to be addressed. Before you can access the maturity level for a business process, the project team first must understand how business solutions evolve, and the key indicators, that the project team should observe.

Understanding Business solution maturity

I do not claim to be a business process management scholar, but allow me to set up some basic premises that we can use as a foundation for our discussion. Broadly, there are three levels of maturity for a business process:

Maturity Level	Description
Initial	The business process can support an execution level where a limited competency can be supported. Key characteristics include inconsistent business activities across different localities, incomplete business process documentation, high error rate, silo technology, and high process costs. Knowledge management is informal at best.
Best Practices	The business process can support an execution level where industry best practices are supported. Key characteristics include a consistent business process model for core activities, competent business process documentation and internal controls, acceptable error rate, integrated technology, and efficient business process costs. Knowledge management is in the early stages (information gathering but inconsistent knowledge capitalization). Business process management and quality initiatives are in place for a subset of business processes.
Competitive	In addition to Best Practices, the business process can support an execution level where country-specific, and industry competitive practices are supported. Key characteristics include a consistent global business process model with variations to support country-specific and industry-specific business activities, complete business process documentation and internal controls, and an effective process model that supports an emerging competitive advantage. Knowledge management is a key driver for business process improvement and enhancing requirements model. Business process management and quality management efforts are corporate standards across the organization.

Let's explore the business process maturity model for a business process (Spend Management) for a Professional Services Automation (PSA) solution. PSA is software designed for professional services organizations, including Consulting and IT services organizations. PSA software is used to manage the delivery of service projects, and the resources that are required for providing the service.

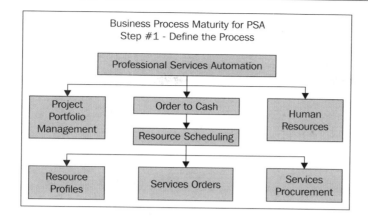

There are many functions involved, but for our purposes, we will focus on the following business activities:

- Project Portfolio Management determines the optimal mix and sequencing of proposed projects to best achieve the organization's overall goals.

- The Order to Cash cycle includes the critical path activities for a professional service organization, including proposal management, project management, resource scheduling, project accounting, and invoicing.

- Human Resources involves all of the activities involved in managing personnel for a professional service organization.

For our discussions, we will focus on the resource scheduling business activity within the Order to Cash business process. The resource scheduling activity is made up of several business tasks. For our discussion we will only focus on the following:

1. Resource Profiles are information on delivery personnel used to assist in resource scheduling. An example of information contained in resource profiles includes skills, accomplishments, project experience, and resumes.

2. Service Orders are request for resources to deliver a service. Information contained in Service Orders includes customer, start and end dates, location, and required skills for the service.

3. Service Procurement identifies, procures, and manages third-party providers (contractors).

As a first step, we will define the high-level business activities. This model includes a comprehensive set of business activities (core, best practice, competitive) — regardless of whether the customer performs these activities today. Even if the scope of the implementation is only focusing on a subset of business activities, the project team cannot ignore the other business activities. This limited view presents difficulties later, when the packaged software is not able to be scaled or expanded due to the initial configuration decisions made.

 Challenge to packaged software providers

Packaged software providers should be able to provide their customers with a complete set of business process models with at least Initial and Best Practice level activities. Leading packaged software partners should also be able to provide industry-specific, country-specific, and competitive business activities in their business model definitions.

Once the project team has defined the first iteration of the business model, the next step is to define the maturity levels where the business activities would be executed. Continuing to expand upon our previous example:

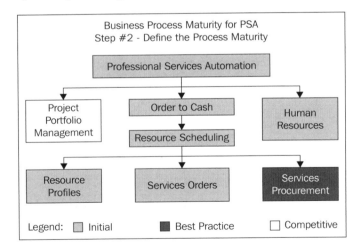

Now, we need to further elaborate. The business activities executing at the Initial business maturity level represent the essential activities required to support the underlying business model. Services Procurement and Project Portfolio Management business activities may be performed, however, these activities are most likely performed inconsistently and manually.

To further progress, we now determine the packaged software feature or component that would support a business activity.

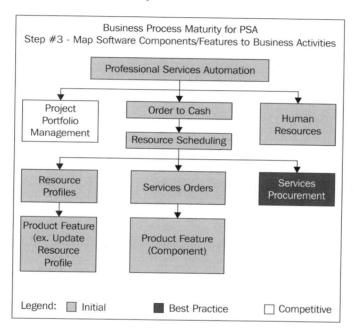

Once we have elaborated the business model to the business software features, the project team will be in a position to identify the features that you need to implement in order to support your current business activities.

Challenge to implementation partners

In general, packaged software providers are offering more functionality within their software products. Figuring out what packaged software features to implement can be a long and difficult process. Implementation partners should recommend to customers a set of packaged software features to implement, based upon the current business maturity level. The earlier you can eliminate product features from a project scope, the more time (and money) you will save the customer. Trusted advisors should lead with a solution.

Within a business process maturity level, there is another dimension that comes into play, which identifies the performance for a business process. The boundaries of this spectrum are typically referred to as efficiency and effectiveness. The majority of customers I have worked with on packaged software implementations wanted a business solution that was both efficient and effective. On the surface, these attributes appear to conflict with one another but that is not the case. The challenge typically arises when you try to address both performance levels at the same time. Lean Six-Sigma is an approach that marries both goals into a logical sequence such that the two goals complement one another. Let's see how these goals can complement one another and how the concepts would apply to a packaged software implementation.

Business process performance within a maturity level

What is the performance level for the underlying business processes that support value generation for the customers? Are the business processes efficient (streamlined, consistent) or effective (proactively identifying customer trends, generating competitive advantage)? It has been my experience that customers like to have both efficient and effective business processes. This approach has usually resulted in defining conflicting business requirements that try to address all of the performance characteristics of a business process at one time.

Some people feel that business process efficiency and effectiveness is an either/ or proposition. Either your business process is efficient or your business process is effective. "Interestingly, organizations implementing Lean Six Sigma products recognize several fundamental truths:

1. Getting faster can actually improve quality.
2. Improving quality can actually make you faster.
3. Reducing complexity improves speed and quality.

However, this cycle doesn't happen unless you apply both Lean and Six Sigma." [2]

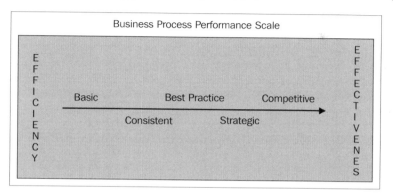

Illustration for a Professional Services Organization

Let's spend a little time and talk about a real life application of efficiency drivers and effectiveness drivers for an industry—Professional Services. For a Professional Services Organization, the service delivery process (i.e., delivery of consulting services) is of utmost importance. How can you determine what the performance level is for the service delivery process? Each business process has their own set of indicators that identify the level of sophistication the customer is at in their service delivery process. Based upon the pains that your customer is currently experiencing, the project team can determine where your customer is on the continuum.

Efficiency pains	Effectiveness pains
No profitability analysis at the project level.	Not proactively identifying market trends and new service opportunities.
High credit rebill rate.	High employee turnover due to ineffective hiring practices.
Focused on saving costs and becoming operational efficient.	Focused on gaining market share and generating competitive advantage.
Receives the request to find the resources to staff the project after the project is sold.	Not developing/managing a resource pool to support future business needs.

Lean Six Sigma promotes the approach of first addressing efficiency then evolving the focus on effectiveness. If the customer does not have some competent level of operational efficiency, then they will only experience a modest or inconsistent level of effectiveness. The best approach is to focus on efficiency and then move towards effectiveness. The implementation partner should give the customer, a roadmap to get to the solution vision described in the sales/procurement process. This roadmap must address not only the customer's existing business process maturity level but also the business process performance level.

> *Rule: Technology alone does not elevate a customer to the next maturity level.*

Technology alone does not make a business solution! The trap with software-focused implementations is that customers see the products available and have expectations of quickly implementing new technology to gain better performance and ROI. However, technology is a small component of a business solution. If the customer does not have the organizational bandwidth or change flexibility to effectively utilize new business process activities, then get ready for a rough ride.

Defining the evolutionary path of a business solution

In order to define a solution vision, we must first understand how a business solution evolves and matures. This requires not only an appreciation of the packaged business software's roadmap but also the underlying business model. Business requirements evolve because the underlying business process evolves—not the technology. Now we will review the following business solution maturity model. Before we discuss this exhibit, let's spend some time defining new key terms that we will reference.

- Lean: Business process improvement methodology that focuses on the following:
    - Maximizing process velocity
    - Provides tools for analyzing process flow and delay times
    - Centres on the separation of value-added from non-value-added work
    - Provides a means for quantifying and eliminating the cost of complexity[3]

- Quality: Quality initiative like Total Quality Management (TQM) or Six Sigma.
- Efficiency: Executing business activities without wasted energy or effort.

- Effectiveness: Producing a desired business result that creates a competitive advantage.

- Business Process Management (BPM) consists of methods, techniques and tools to design, deploy, control, and analyze operational business processes involving humans, organizations, applications, documents, and other sources of information.

- Business Process Reengineering is the rapid and radical redesign of strategic, value-added business processes — and the systems, policies, and organizational structures that support them — in order to optimize the work flows and productivity in an organization.[4]

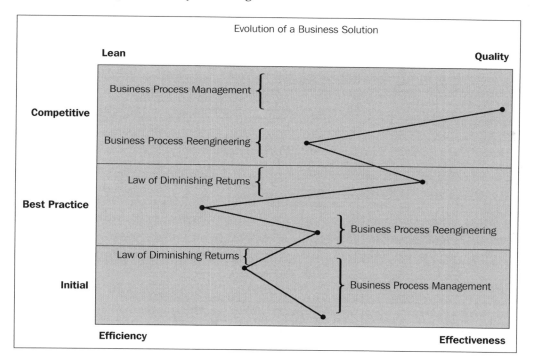

For this narrative, we will use a fictitious Professional Services Organization called Trusted Advisors Consulting (TAC). TAC is addressing their needs for an enterprise business solution. Current business processes are a hodge-podge of point applications, spreadsheets, and "inconsistent" business rules.

Initial level

When TAC first implements a packaged business solution, their business process execution is neither efficient nor effective. TAC only implemented the software functionality that supported current business activities. The business process maturity level is supporting — at best. After the initial implementation, TAC should focus on business process efficiency, as recommended by Lean Six Sigma. Naturally, as the users gain additional experience with their business solution, they will become more efficient. TAC develops and implements a business process management program to address business process performance and maturity.

Time has passed and TAC has made great strides with their business process management program. TAC has noted that it is taking more and more resources to squeeze additional efficiency from their business processes. TAC is experiencing the Law of Diminishing Returns. In addition, the business is experiencing limitations (boundary pains) due to the limited functionality provided by its current COTS software configuration. TAC can either deal with the limitations or evolve to the next maturity level. Unlike incremental process improvement within a maturity level, moving to the next maturity level will require a breakout effort by the business. New business activities will emerge and existing business activities may change. The effort required will be more of a re-engineering initiative versus an incremental process improvement initiative.

Best Practice level

The only area available to TAC in order to drastically improve their business process execution is to focus on business process effectiveness. As TAC now focuses on effectiveness, they investigate and implement new packaged software functionality that supports business activity, which would occur within the basic business process maturity level.

As Michael George pointed out — people could get complacent: you want every employee to feel the pressure of continuous improvement.[5] Unfortunately, most people equate improvement to specialization. I challenged my customers to view this statement in terms of broadening themselves across a business solution. As TAC moves to the Best Practice maturity level, they will once again go through the efficiency to effectiveness performance path. As business process performance matures, TAC will once again feel the boundary pains associated with their current business solution.

Competitive practice level

This is an area where the customer does work efficiently and also performs the correct work in order to maximize business value. However, this may also be the area where we experience the most gaps with the packaged software. It is at this point where your relationship with IT, Implementation Partners, and the packaged software provider could have a significant impact on the customer's Total Cost of Ownership (TCO). IT, Implementation Partners, and the packaged software provider also have a great opportunity to generate tremendous business value, as well as create competitive advantage for themselves. Having a "Partner-Partner" relationship will generate opportunities, shared efforts, and reduced Total Cost of Ownership. Having a "Customer-Vendor" relationship will generate competing agendas, frustrations, missed opportunities, and higher Total Cost of Ownership.

 ### Challenge to implementation partners and customers

Do customers need revenue-generating business processes operating at a competitive level? I believe that we would all agree that the answer is yes. Do customers need revenue-supporting business processes operating at a competitive level? In theory, the majority of us would say no; however, the reality is that conflict will arise between what is best for the entire organization versus what is best for a functional area. Customers that are organized into functional units will naturally look for new functionality and define new requirements to improve their functional performance. Too often, I have seen customers make significant software changes to packaged software in order to support a competitive or "world class" maturity level for revenue supporting business processes. These decisions have resulted in software that is not adaptable, and that costs more to maintain than the legacy system it replaced.

Implementation partners need to guide their customers to ensure that there is alignment between business user expectations and the executives' expectations on using packaged software This alignment must be continually communicated and demonstrated throughout the packaged software implementation.

Not every business process should mature to a competitive level. In theory, one should see strategic business processes become Competitive, while supporting business processes operate at a Best Practice level. Practically speaking, it is very challenging to be the best at everything because our focus will be diluted.

To be a true business solution advisor, we must understand what makes your customer successful, and then make an investment to help your customer be successful. This will require the implementation partner to understand what business activities of a revenue-supporting business process add value to the external customer, as well as what business activities may not have a significant impact on the external customer. It is impossible for the implementation partner to evaluate and challenge business requirements if the implementation partner does not understand the business.

It is very important that customers select an implementation partner who have a competent level of knowledge in both the packaged software and the underlying business model. I have witnessed, on many occasions, consultants with packaged software knowledge inappropriately using packaged software to support a business process. This was due to the lack of business process knowledge and understanding. This misuse resulted in a business solution that was inflexible and costly. For some instances the only way to correct the issue was a reimplementation. Finding an implementation partner with competent experience in both the packaged software and underlying business model may cost more, but given the possible risk defined above, I believe that it's worth the cost; there are other ways to save money on packaged software implementations.

Now we will discuss three broad categories of business processes and how to approach requirements gathering for each category.

Three broad categories of business processes

I simply look at business processes in terms of generating revenue—the life source for a company. Business processes generate revenue, support revenue generation, or are mandated by a legal entity or institution.

Revenue generating

To remain competitive in this increasingly-shrinking world, organizations are continually faced with challenges to reduce product development time, improve product quality, and reduce product costs and lead time. One challenge of customer-facing, revenue-generating business processes is that they show high variation in demand, resulting in evolving requirements. Market share and potential growth are linked to getting the right product to the right place at the right time. Referring back to our Professional Service Organization example in the previous section, the Order to Cash process would be a revenue generating business process.

From an implementation perspective, the following are the underlying drivers to consider:

- Target maturity level is competitive
- More focus on effectiveness than efficiency
- Higher tolerance for business risk
- Rapid development (time to market)
- Spend money to make money
- Business requirements will be evolving
- Business scenarios will have multiple variations (pushing against consistency)

Revenue supporting

Revenue-supporting business processes are those business processes that *support* the revenue-generating business processes. Referring back to our Professional Service Organization example in the previous section, the Human Resources process would be a revenue-supporting business process. The majority of revenue-supporting business processes should focus on a Best Practice maturity level. Market drivers are supporting this concept with the growth of the business process outsourcing market (BPO). BPO allows companies to both support non-revenue-generating business processes at a Best Practice level, and free up resources to focus on maturing the revenue-generating business processes.

From an implementation perspective, the following are the underlying drivers to consider:

- Target maturity level is Best Practice
- Business requirements should be relatively steady
- Medium tolerance for business risk
- More focus on efficiency than effectiveness
- Reducing cost is paramount
- Drive efficiency by reducing business process variations. Variations should occur in relation to locality, regulatory, and compliance requirements.

Regulatory and compliance

Regulatory and compliance business processes are activities required for a company to operate within a specific regulatory area or locality. An example of regulatory and compliance processes is Sarbanes Oxley.

From an implementation perspective, the following are the underlying drivers to consider:

- No tolerance for business risk
- More focus on efficiency than effectiveness
- Reducing cost is paramount
- Requirements should be steady. Regulatory/compliance agencies are not considered to be rapidly-evolving entities.

Understanding how business solutions change and evolve are key in determining the correct implementation approach for the customer. Now that we have established the context, let's discuss the recommendation of implementing to the current level in further detail.

Best Practice—Implement to the current maturity level

The approach of implementing to the current business process maturity level of the customer creates a healthy balance between technology, business processes, people, and project risk. It focuses on minimizing the impact to the component (people) , and maximizing the impact on a business solution. This approach also puts the project team in a position to reap early success. In the following sections we will outline the key benefits with this approach.

Minimize evolving business requirements

Managing evolving business requirements can be a significant challenge in any implementation, and can present a significant risk. Let's briefly examine the key drivers for evolving business requirements:

1. Requirements support customer-facing, revenue-generating business process.
2. Requirements support a new business activity for the customer. The customer has no organizational history or an agreed-upon business construct to derive requirements.

It's worth repeating that there is a difference between truly evolving requirements (i.e., the business model changes) and the project team having an evolving understanding of the requirements. Implementing to the current business process maturity will reduce evolving business requirements. Project scope can be easily understood (focus on what the customer performs today). There will always be business processes and/activities where the project team will encounter evolving requirements. However, the project team should minimize evolving business requirements wherever possible—especially where the customer does not perform the business activity today. Evolving business requirements involve more effort and greater risk. The risk may be worth it for a revenue-generating business process but is less desirable for a revenue-supporting or compliance business process.

Minimize organizational change

Implementing to the current business process maturity also minimizes the organizational change associated with a new business solution. The undeniable fact is that a packaged software application will change how business is done. Also, consider that the majority of customers do not have an extensive amount of experience with implementing "off-the-shelf" software. These changes result in a significant learning curve for both Business and IT. Sticking to the current business process activities will eliminate the need for Business and IT to learn new business activities and related software functionality.

Maximize opportunity for rapid delivery

Implementing to the current business process maturity puts the project team in a better position to generate business value faster. Minimizing change allows the project team to move quicker and generate project momentum faster. Nothing promotes adoption like success!

Summary

If you had the opportunity to reduce implementation risk and be able to generate business value faster, would you do it? Reducing risk and accelerating business value are the underlying drivers for implementing to the current business process maturity level.

One of the most critical areas that is extremely hard to manage is organizational impact. Implementing at the current business process maturity level helps to minimize the organizational impact. Implementing at the current business process maturity level also assists in limiting the impact to the customer's value chain network (business partners, suppliers, joint ventures, and so on).

Customers naturally look to address the maximum set of requirements they can implement given their investment (i.e., get the most bang for their buck). The challenge to all of us who call ourselves IT and Implementation Partners must be to act as business solution advisors and develop the correct mix of people, processes, and technology to develop a successful business solution.

However, it is hard to be viewed as a business solution advisor if we do not know the underlying business model and how business solutions change and mature. Having this knowledge is fundamental to enabling IT and Implementation Partners to provide the guidance that the Business needs in order to correctly apply technology. Business solution implementations always involve risks. The key is to find the approach that allows the project team to maximize business value yet take smart business risks and minimize pure risks. Implementing to the current business maturity level is a great place to start in defining the correct approach for the business solution implementation. In the next chapter, we will discuss a software change strategy for COTS software that will minimize potential risks and maximize opportunities for additional software value.

Reference

1. Ross, Ronald, *Principles of the Business Rules Approach*. Addison-Wesley, 2003, Page 105.

2. George, Michael L., *Lea n Six Sigma for Services*. McGraw-Hill, 2003, Page 6.

3. George, Michael L., *Lean Six Sigma for Services*. McGraw-Hill, 2003, Page 7.

4. Manganelli, Raymond L. and Klein, Mark M., *The Reengineering Handbook*. AMACOM, 1994, Page 7.

5. George, Michael L., *Lean Six Sigma for Services*. McGraw-Hill, 2003, Page 59.

8

Minimizing Customizations and Maximizing Enhancements

How You Gather Requirements Sends a Message!

Let's us go through an analogy together. You are the customer and I am the consultant working with you to develop some software changes for your packaged software. As the consultant, I can take two approaches for gathering requirements:

- *Option #1: "What would you like?"* An open-ended question that will generate a lot of feedback from you, the customer. Yet, it communicates several underlying messages:
  - ° You will get a customized solution. Software changes require minimal effort.
  - ° I, as the consultant, may not have sufficient knowledge of your business—or not enough to lead with a recommendation.
  - ° You, the customer, know exactly what you want.
  - ° I, as the consultant, appear to be more customer-focused.

- *Option #2: "Here is the delivered functionality. Please explain why this is not sufficient."* A question that will generate less feedback from you, the customer. Yet, it communicates several underlying messages:
  - ° You may not get what you want. Software changes should not be required.
  - ° I, as the consultant, may not have sufficient knowledge of your business—especially if I did not know of the gaps beforehand.

- ○ You may feel that you have been put on the defensive and not treated appropriately as the key stakeholder.
  - ○ I, as the consultant, appear to be less customer-focused.

- *Option #3: "How is your current system configured today to support your business?"* A question that the customer will easily be able to answer in the shortest amount of time. Yet, it communicates several underlying messages:
  - ○ You will get exactly what you have today—both the good and the bad.
  - ○ I, as the consultant, may be looking to minimize the amount of effort required to set up a new packaged software.
  - ○ I, as the consultant, appear to be more customer-focused.

All of the above options are valid approaches for gathering requirements. However, the challenges I am seeing today are due to how project teams apply requirements gathering strategies to their packaged software implementations. Project teams confine themselves to one approach and do not account for the challenges associated with the selected method. Following are definitions of the three key requirements-gathering strategies for packaged software.

Requirements-driven strategy

A pure requirements-driven strategy focuses on defining all business requirements independent of organizational and technological constraints. This approach is the most widely-used method today. This is also the slowest approach to gathering requirements and will require the most time from the Business to articulate the requirements. We can anticipate gathering non-value-added business requirements that must be filtered through the requirements selection process. With additional gaps, the Business will have to spend more during Fit/Gap to make decisions.

Solution-driven strategy

On the other end of the spectrum, a pure solution-driven strategy focuses on the gap business requirements (requirements that cannot be met with the delivered functionality). This approach is highly popular in an accelerated implementation method. This approach requires the least amount of time from the Business; however, the Business must conform to the packaged business software. This could have a significant impact on organizational acceptance and impact because packaged software designs are based upon a market-driven set of requirements and not the specific requirements of an individual customer.

Configuration-driven strategy

The configuration-driven strategy is based upon the premise "The new system needs to do what the existing system does today". It may be a situation where a customer simply needs a replacement system because the existing system is nearing the end of its license and may become decommissioned software. Starting with what the customer knows helps to expedite requirements gathering. Business time is minimized because IT can provide insight into the existing business system capabilities and configuration. However, this approach will raise requirements based upon existing system limitations as well as legacy non-value-added business requirements.

Let's summarize the requirements management strategies for packaged business software.

Strategy	Advantages	Disadvantages
Requirements-driven	• Comprehensive requirements model • Customer feels like they are being heard	• Identify more non-critical gaps • Gather requirements based upon existing system design and limitations • Slower business requirements gathering
Solution-driven	• Focus on critical path requirements • Puts responsibilities on customer • Accelerates business requirements gathering	• Customer feels that needs are not being met • Customer is forced to take what is there • Potential for greater organizational change and risk of acceptance

Strategy	Advantages	Disadvantages
Configuration-driven	• Point of reference that the customer intimately knows • Customer feels like they are being listened to • Identify the exceptional-based cases by reviewing existing customer configurations	• Implementation partner needs to bridge the gap • Gather requirements based upon existing system design and limitations

As important as requirements gathering is, it is only one activity in the requirements management process. As the implementation team selects the requirement-gathering strategy for packaged software, it is important to ensure the team also considers the other requirements management activities as well.

Requirements management revisited

When the topic of business requirements is mentioned, most people think about gathering requirements. I have observed several projects where significant effort was spent in gathering requirements but the project failed to adequately address the other areas of requirements management. A key problem noted is performing requirements selection before requirements validation. Following are the key activities for effective requirements management:

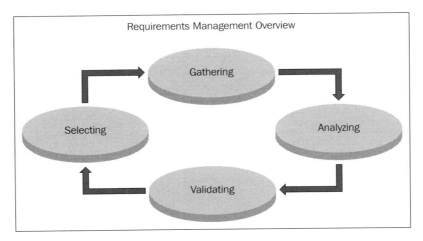

Requirements management is more about understanding the business and the strategic direction of the customer's business—not just a point-in-time assessment. Requirements management is an on-going process that enables the customer to be more flexible, which is key for business process improvement. To truly understand the customer's business processes, we need to understand the value-added business requirements. To ensure that we are on the same page, We will spend some time in briefly defining each requirements management area:

Gathering requirements

Gathering requirements is the first step in requirements management. There are several methods available for gathering requirements:

- **Interviewing**: A functional consultant from the implementation partner will work with the customer's business experts to gather requirements. The functional consultant will utilize a set of questions based on the packaged software functionality (i.e., product questionnaire) to solicit requirements.

- **Joint Application Development (JAD) session**: A JAD session is a series of working sessions where representatives from Business, IT, and the Implementation Partner come together to define requirements. JAD sessions allow different perspectives to be given on requirements as well as encourage interaction between the key project team players.

- **Prototyping**: Prototyping involves using the packaged software as a vehicle to help define requirements. These sessions are typically known as "conference room pilots".

- **Use Cases** (storyboarding): Use Cases are a description of a system's behavior as it responds to a request that originates from outside of that system. In other words, a use case describes "who" can do "what" with the system in question.

The question is not "Which method is the best to use?" but rather "What combination of methods should I use?" Audience, business time constraints, and business requirement stability are all factors that the project team must consider to identify the correct method(s). Do not limit yourself to one method for defining requirements. The more methods (perspectives) you employ to gather requirements, the greater the probability for success, because the project team will have the opportunity to understand requirements from all angles (input, processing, outputs). Later in this chapter, I will demonstrate how to best use these methods when gathering requirements for packaged software.

Analyzing requirements

Analyzing requirements focuses on reviewing the defined requirements to ensure that they are complete and understandable to all project team members. Ambiguous, contradictory, or incomplete business requirements should be resolved. A key analysis to perform is comparing the customer's requirements with a standard set of business requirements for a specific business area.

 Challenge to implementation partners

Implementation partners should consider having a standard definition of key business requirements for a business process based upon their experience with assisting their customers' packaged software implementations. This set of common requirements can compared against the current set of customer requirements to ensure completeness.

Validating requirements

Validating requirements includes making sure that the project team correctly heard the customer. Typical requirements validation activities include:

1. **Peer Reviews**: Peer reviews are where peer(s) review the defined requirements and provide updates to ensure that the requirements definitions are complete. It is important to note that this technique is only as good as the peer(s) who are reviewing the requirements.

2. **Business Solution Modeling**: Business solution modeling is executing business scenarios against a working, realistic version of the packaged software. This activity takes place before the fit/gap sessions. Please refer to Chapter 4 for additional information.

3. **Test Cases**: A test case includes a set of inputs, actions, and expected outputs to determine whether the software is working correctly or not.

A best implementation practice is to use multiple methods to validate business requirements. In general, the more chances one gives oneself to hit the target, the greater the probability for success.

Selecting requirements

One of the most popular methods for selecting business requirements from customers is to hold individual fit/gap session(s) for each software product or feature set. A walkthrough of the packaged business software functionality and configuration is reviewed with "fits" and "gaps" identified. These fits and gaps are captured in a document. The team focuses on the gaps to determine whether the gap will be addressed by one of the following methods:

- Software (customization or enhancement)
- Business process change (conform to the software)
- Postpone to a future release or phase
- Drop the requirement from consideration

During the selection process, gaps will be prioritized to facilitate how the gap will be addressed.

When it comes to packaged software, project teams have a difficult time with requirements management because most rely on a traditional "build from scratch" mentality that does not take full advantage of delivered functionality. Traditional approaches for gathering requirements for packaged business software maximizes the identifications of gaps. A technology (software) focused implementation approach will naturally encourage using software as the means of addressing gaps. We assume that every business requirement will add value and that the underlying business processes are fully optimized. There is no effort to reset expectations on the business software. If the project team do reset expectations, then the team is in a losing battle. There should be a balance between the functionality that the software offers and the objectives for the customer's business model. Finding that balance begins with having an approach that appreciates the different drivers involved in selecting packaged software in the first place.

The following section will describe a requirements management strategy that encourages customers to maximize their packaged software investment.

Value-added requirements management

What if there was a way to take the best from all of the approaches mentioned above and produce a strategy that took full advantage of packaged software? What if we could bring in different approaches in such way as to complement and progressively elaborate (iterate) business requirements? This is the aim of the blended approach—to leverage different techniques in the process where they can generate the most value. The project team gathers business requirements from different perspectives, which enables the team to create a holistic requirements definition set. Finally, the approach will naturally filter out non-value-added business requirements. Let's review how we would execute a blended approach for requirements gathering.

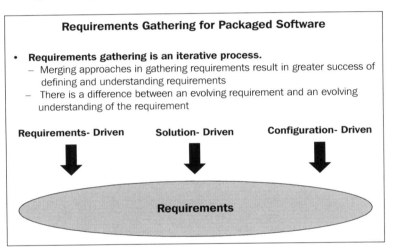

Iteration #1 – listen to the customer

In the first iteration, we will utilize the requirements-driven approach to gather high-level requirements. The difference in applying this approach is the level or degree that we execute in this iteration. The objective is to gather **enough** business requirements to allow the project team to develop a competent system for business solution modeling. A key concept here is that your customer needs to feel that they are being listened to and engaged, yet not being promised a custom solution. The project team wants to be able to develop a system that will **convince** the customer that the packaged software will support their business. Focus on gathering the main business scenarios and relevant data that will enable the project team to produce a realistic solution to utilize during business solution modeling.

Iteration #2 – Lead the customer

Here, the project team transitions from listening to leading, with a business solution. During business solution modeling, the project team will demonstrate to the customers the ability of the packaged software to support the main business scenarios. During business solution modeling, the project team also focuses on gathering exceptions to the standard business process scenarios defined. You will also note that this activity will provide the project team with the opportunity to **validate** business requirements and software configuration **during** the requirements gathering process.

Iteration #3 – Confirm with the customer

This final iteration is a confirmation that all value-added business requirements are defined and all business exceptions and scenarios have been addressed. Looking at the configuration of your customer's legacy system(s) not only is another source of validation but can also be the first iteration of defining legacy data migration requirements.

Challenging business requirements

Requirements selection is one of the most important activities that the project team will face during an implementation. And at the end of the day, the customer will have the final say regarding what business requirements will be selected and what method (business process change, automation) will be used. The implementation partner will be key in helping their customer to evaluate and challenge business requirements, to ensure that the customer gets maximum business value at minimal cost and risk.

 Challenge to implementation partners

The first step in being considered a trusted advisor is to have a solid understanding of the customer's business model. Keep in mind that you will never know more about the business than the customer. However, you should have a firm understanding of the standard business scenarios and work flows. The implementation partner's job is not to select requirements for the customer but rather to facilitate discussions with the customer to examine business requirements that cannot be addressed via delivered packaged software functionality.

Customizations versus enhancements

Some may say that there is no difference between customizations and enhancements. Others say that customizations are software changes to existing packaged software functionality and enhancements are software changes to create new functionality. I firmly believe that there is a difference between customizations and enhancements but that definition is oriented towards value-added and non-value-added software changes.

What are customizations?

Customizations are software changes to packaged software that address non-value-added requirements — it is a business requirement that supports a business activity that adds no value to the final business result. Customizations may also be software changes to address software bugs in the existing packaged software.

Generally speaking, customizations are software changes where the packaged software provider is not interested in partnering with customers because the software change does not offer an opportunity to differentiate their packaged software. Packaged software providers are successful if they can sell more software.

What are enhancements?

Enhancements are changes to packaged software that generate **material** business value for a customer. Generally speaking, enhancements are software changes where the packaged software provider is potentially interested in partnering with the project team because the software change can generate business value across a broad audience (and enables them sell more software). Revisiting our business process maturity model, we can see where business requirements generally fall and how packaged software usually supports the defined requirements.

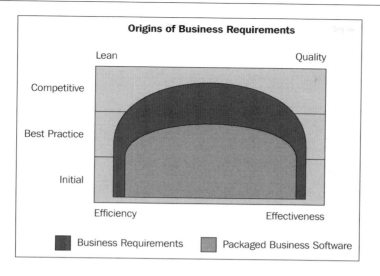

Where would we find the business requirements that would add the most value to your business? If the customer has selected a competent packaged software, then the business software should provide "out of the box" functionality to address the majority of business requirements at the *Initial* and *Best Practice* maturity levels (see Chapter 7). It is rare to have a packaged business solution provide complete coverage of all Best Practice requirements. However, there will always be competitive requirements that are not addressed by the COTS software.

I will now add to the previous model to represent enhancements and customizations:

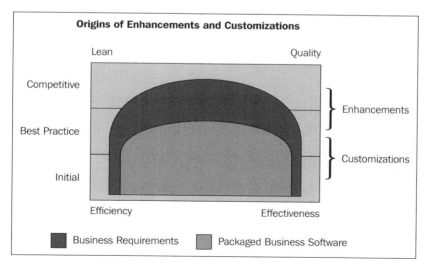

Repeatedly, I have witnessed project teams struggle with the lower-level requirements and run out of time when collecting higher-level requirements. By blending requirement gathering strategies, the project team can encourage the customer to (a) fully utilize delivered functionality, and (b) focus on the enhancements that will generate maximum value for your business.

 Case Study

I was a project manager leading requirements gathering and fit/gap sessions for a new implementation of packaged business software for a defense manufacturing company. The customer had an aggressive timeframe. To remain on project schedule, we needed to perform requirements gathering and conduct a formal fit/gap for 15 COTS software products in eight weeks (normal duration is sixteen weeks). We did an initial gap analysis and identified seventy-five possible software changes. If we used a traditional, requirements-driven approach then (a) we would have been over-schedule/over-budget and (b) the number of software changes would increase due to existing business software expectations.

The approach we took was to focus on gathering the critical path, value-added business requirements, and make a concerted effort to leverage delivered functionality. We also required that a formal business case was developed for each gap requirement. Most important was the strategy of changing perceptions and how best to leverage packaged software. At the beginning of every working session, we spent five to ten minutes to expound upon the principles outlined in this book.

The existing legacy system that we were replacing was a packaged software product. The customer's initial implementation focused on delivering a highly-customized solution using a traditional implementation approach. Over the next ten years, additional customizations were made that further limited the COTS software investment. Eventually, the customer decided to replace the existing COTS software because it would cost less to implement new software than to upgrade the existing software in-house. What was needed was a "game-changing" approach. Otherwise, the customer might end up right back at the same spot with no new business value to show for it.

The key result from the above approach was that the project team was able to reduce software changes by 45%! Reduced software changes means a faster implementation, lower Total Cost of Ownership, and allows the customer to leverage new packaged software functionality quicker via upgrades. Most important to note is that these results would not have been possible without making the investment in the project team (Business, IT, Implementation Partner) to have a common understanding and language to effectively collaborate.

Challenges and risks with valued-added requirements management

It is important to highlight some of the key challenges with the requirements management blended approach described above. First, is the assumption that the selected packaged business reasonably addresses Initial and Best Practice level business requirements. It is important to ensure that there is an adequate fit between the packaged software functionality and the customer's business model. Otherwise, additional time and effort is required by the project team to perform effective requirements management activities. If the project team has to worry about packaged software supporting basic business requirements, then the implementation has far bigger challenges to address.

Second, the approach is people-dependent. The blended strategy assumes that the project team have competent IT personnel and Implementations Partner consultants who have hands-on experience or formal training in the packaged business solution being implemented. What is most critical is the appropriate Business representation. The Business subject matter experts should have a deep knowledge of their business model and its variations. This approach will encourage Business representatives to proactively filter existing non-value-added business requirements, and the Business representatives should have the authority to do so.

Finally, this approach will result in additional organizational change versus taking a traditional requirements-driven approach. For a moment, let's step back and take a strategic view of this challenge, referring back to our definition of a business solution.

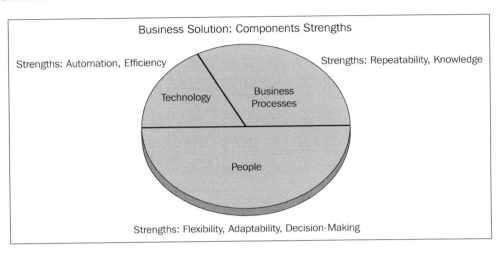

The key decision to make during fit/gap is whether people will change or will the software change. Which one is more flexible and adaptable? Packaged software can be flexible and adaptable given the project team has the resources and effort required to adapt the software. Keep in mind that people have a greater capacity to adapt and change. It's important that you make decisions with the goal of leveraging the individual components appropriately in order to maximize their core strengths. This is especially relevant for gaps that would be addressed via software customizations (low business value).

None of the above assumptions and challenges is unrealistic; however, it is important to remember that the approach defined above must be tailored for the implementation.

Summary

Every packaged software implementation will require software changes. By definition, every software change will result in a high Total Cost of Ownership for the customer. As software changes increase, the greater the resource requirements needed to perform a packaged software upgrade. Packaged software upgrades are the primary means for customers to leverage new functionality. Not being in a position to quickly upgrade may result in losing competitive advantage, and wasting money paid on maintenance fees.

Using a blended approach to gathering requirements for packaged business software enables the project team to be responsive to the customer yet encourage the customer to utilize delivered functionality to its fullest. It is an approach that focuses only on software changes that generate maximum business value and return on investment.

A fundamental premise that supports all the other principles described in this book is the ability to negotiate. In the next chapter, we will outline the negotiation strategy required for implementing COTS software that will maximize the ownership experience.

9

Negotiate for Success

Executive sponsorship is not enough!

Having effective executive sponsorship is a key success factor for any business solution implementation. There are countless books and presentations that have communicated this best practice to the marketplace. Executive sponsorship may guarantee financial support but it does not guarantee organizational acceptance and adoption.

For example, Panorama Consulting conducted a study of 2008 ERP implementations from over one thousand organizations across the globe. The study focused on the top ERP challenges. Respondents indicated that lack of employee adoption as the biggest challenge (33%). Surprisingly, not a single respondent identified lack of executive support as the biggest problem.

Trickle down acceptance falls short

A key assumption made on several packaged software implementations is that if the executive management selects Commercial Off The Shelf (COTS) software, then the organization would adopt the executive's intentions. When executive management selects packaged software, they are making the following statement:

A custom software solution is not strategic for the organization.

It is interesting to note that the above statement is not publicly reiterated throughout the life of the implementation project. It's like a little secret that is implied but hardly repeated. Unfortunately, the key business process owners and other stakeholders do not always respond to "trickle down" acceptance. Their expectation is based on their past software experience, which is usually getting what they want without any questions asked. Packaged software makes for an expensive custom solution. If the project team does not reset existing business software expectations, then it will be extremely difficult to be successful. If the project team makes no software changes and use packaged software as delivered then end user adoption and satisfaction will be harder to develop. If the project team focuses on building a custom solution then the Total Cost of Ownership (TCO) will be significant and will result in less executive satisfaction due to the increased cost. Successful COTS software implementations are those that are able to balance (negotiate) tradeoffs that result in minimizing TCO and maximizing organizational acceptance.

The following section will discuss the key areas that the project team should address as part of their negotiation strategy.

Developing an effective negotiation strategy

An effective negotiation strategy for packaged software implementations is where all parties are aligned in supporting the success of the implementation. It is also important for the project team to perform certain activities to promote alignment and adoption. The first step in developing an effective negotiation strategy is to establish realistic expectations to close the gap between custom software and packaged software.

Paradigm shift in business software expectations

One of the key mindsets that the project team have to make with the stakeholders and end users are expectations of business software. Typically, stakeholders and end users see business software as a simple tool that can easily be adapted to support their activities. It is rare for stakeholders and end users to understand the complete ramifications of their requests. There are times when stakeholders and end users do not care to know what efforts are required to make the business software do exactly what they want. Regardless of the underlying drivers, the project team must make the effort to educate and influence stakeholders and end users to develop areas of compromise.

Case Study

I was the functional consulting lead for a packaged software application to replace a customer's legacy time reporting system. The customer's process consisted of electronic spreadsheets coupled together with a data load process to a staging table for payroll processing. When I started working with the customer to define their business requirements, it was apparent that there was a difference between executive and business stakeholder expectations. The customer insisted on having the exact functionality that they had in their existing systems. I knew that no matter how good the developers were, we would not be able to cost-effectively build the existing flexibility into the packaged software. It would totally invalidate the justification for going with a packaged software solution in the first place. The customer was used to getting exactly what they wanted from software to the point where software replaced the need for training (i.e., dummy-proofing). I did an initial gap analysis and identified over forty (40) gaps that required changes to the packaged software.

I came to the realization that if I proceeded with a traditional approach to gathering requirements that: (a) I would spend a lot of wasted effort gathering non-value-added business requirements and (b) the fit/gap session would be much longer than anticipated. It was a no-win situation. The best approach was to reset software expectations with the customer up-front. I met with the customer to discuss the reasons for selecting packaged software and the inherent advantages and disadvantages with packaged software. This was not a one-time discussion and required several additional discussions.

In the end, the customer's expectations adapted, which enabled us to accelerate our fit/gap session. We still identified ten gaps. Of the ten gaps, we negotiated to have only five addressed via a software change and the other five gaps were handled manually due to the frequency of occurrence. Our negotiations resulted in an 87% reduction from the initial estimate and were only made possible by establishing a suitable environment for effective negotiating. If either party has unrealistic expectations then effective negotiations would have been extremely difficult.

Paradigm shift in organizational acceptance

The second paradigm shift that the project team has to make is in how to gain organizational acceptance. This area is addressed in organizational change management. Organizational Change Management is good at defining the tactical steps that you need to perform in **preparing** the organization for a new business solution. However, a more aggressive approach needs to be taken. The **entire** project team needs to **sell** the solution to the organization. I'm talking about a concerted effort—no soft selling here. The project team needs to have real influence with the stakeholders and end users. The project team needs to lead discussions with stakeholders and key end users; negotiating a business solution that balances their needs (not wants) with the strategy of using packaged software. The project team needs to persuade their customers that they have the customer's best interests at heart and will produce a competent business solution.

Understand when and where to negotiate

Negotiating on business requirements is a certainty that must be planned for by the project team. The majority of projects do not have a proactive strategy in place to negotiate with stakeholders on business requirements that are not satisfied by the delivered packaged software. Many projects take a reactive approach to negotiating business requirements. This approach typically results in confusion, analysis paralysis, and decisions that undermine the objectives of selecting packaged business software. Following are the key points that the project team needs to address in understanding potential areas for negotiation:

1. Identify areas within the packaged software where software changes are typically made by customers. With the correct implementation partner, the project team may have the opportunity to leverage their software change library to streamline the modification efforts. With the correct packaged software provider, you may have the opportunity to partner together and share the development effort.

2. Identify areas within the packaged software where software changes will have minimal Total Cost of Ownership impact. For example, making a software changes to generate an exception report has less of an impact than building a new application page or process. Determine where the business software provider provides the most support for software changes within their application and lead with these options in the negotiations. For example, reporting is an area that most packaged software providers anticipate their customers modifying, and provide tools and templates for streamlined development and upgrades in this area.

3. Identify areas within the packaged software where software changes will have an adverse impact to the Total Cost of Ownership. For example, software modifications to compiled executables can have several downstream impacts to other components within the packaged software. These software changes can not only negatively impact the Total Cost of Ownership but can also result in unstable business software, and invalidate software support and quality agreements. It is also important for the project team to understand the boundaries of the technical constraints inherent with the packaged software.

4. Determine what to challenge and what to accept regarding business requirements not supported by the packaged software. In general, the project team should focus on maximizing enhancements and minimizing customizations. In the case where customizations must be addressed for project success, implement the customizations with the least impact to the Total Cost of Ownership.

As the project team engages the key stakeholders and end users, do not lead with the functional areas that the team plans to address via software changes. Allow the stakeholders and end users to justify the reasons for negotiating and building software changes. What I learned from these software negotiations is that every party needs to perceive that they have won something. In theory, one can look at this as an inefficient process; however, it reflects human nature and a certain reality that the project team must address. The project team, should as well deal with these types of negotiations in a practical manner. Too often, I have witnessed project teams get stuck in theoretical absolutes that add no business value and slow down the project.

Utilize your packaged software provider

A true partner is someone who is interested in other's success. Therefore, it is reasonable to expect that the packaged software provider is interested in the success of the customer's implementation and should be making investments to ensure implementation success. For example: the customer is making an investment in the success of the packaged software provider by paying for license and maintenance fees. However, it is important that the customer leverage their packaged software partners effectively. A deep software discount does not improve the customer's chances for implementation success. What is required is an analysis of the short-term and long-term opportunities for which the packaged software provider can partner with the customer, in order to ensure a successful implementation.

Short-term opportunities are those activities (investments) that your packaged software can provide to assist the customer during the initial implementation.

Leveraging Packaged Software Partners	
Short-Term	**Long-Term**
• Software configuration best practices across customer base • Collaborate with similar customers • Quick-start Implementation guides & tools • Co-development of key software enhancements • Beta customer program	• Opportunity to include enhancements into core product • Access to product strategy and development • Strategy whitepapers on industry best practices and best practice configurations

Following is a brief overview of the key short-term investments that the packaged software partner can make in order to increase business implementation success:

- **Software configuration best practices** – doing things from scratch costs more than starting with a predefined configuration model. One strategic advantage of a packaged software provider is their customer base. Within the customer base is a wealth of knowledge and experience regarding best practices in utilizing the provider's COTS software. The packaged software provider should glean these configuration best practices from their existing customer base and develop guidance to aid new customers. Providing this configuration guidance will enable customers to accelerate their implementations and generate Return on Investment (ROI) faster.

- **Collaborate with similar customers** – having the ability to collaborate with other customers who have already implemented the packaged software is another resource where new customers can identify possible challenges early in their implementations, and plan for these appropriately.

- **Quick-start implementation guides and tools** – is not a call to replace implementation partners. However, it provides a starting point which will enable the customer to (a) implement faster and (b) be better prepared in order to fully leverage their implementation partner when they are engaged.

- **Co-development of key software enhancement** – is not about getting free software development. It is an approach that provides greater assurance that the customer's software enhancements will have a longer lifecycle. It promotes better alignment with the future direction of the packaged software product.

- **Beta-customer program** – is a great opportunity to accelerate rapid delivery of new functionality in a shared-risk environment.

Following is an overview of the key long-term investments that your packaged software provider can make to increase the chance of continued business implementation success:

- **Opportunity to include enhancements into core product** – is a key value proposition for going with COTS software. However, it will require the customer to develop a compelling sales pitch to the packaged software provider. If the customer can show a broad audience for the software enhancement, then the packaged software provider will likely be more interested. Remember that to be a partner means that the customer is interested in the success of their partners. Selling more software and retaining existing software customers is a key success factor for the packaged software provider.

- **Access to product strategy and development** – is the opportunity that the customer needs in order to develop and foster the partnership. Being aligned with the COTS product strategy organization provides the customer with insight into the opportunities for co-development and influence over future software product direction.

- **Strategy whitepapers on industry best practices and best practice configurations** – provide the thought leadership needed in this hyper-demanding world. Packaged software providers cannot develop software to support a successful business solution if they do not understand the business. When the customer selected a packaged software provider, they were selecting an organization that had a deep appreciation of the underlying business model and leading best practices. It is this knowledge that enables packaged software providers to develop best-of-breed business software.

An effective negotiation strategy for packaged software requires the project team to ensure that the packaged software provider is an active participant during the implementation—not just during the sales/procurement cycle.

A reality that we all must accept is that it is better to negotiate from a position of power. In the next section, we will review key tactics the project team can undertake in order to ensure successful negotiations.

Ensuring successful negotiations

Please note that the following recommendations focus on building a cooperative environment for successful negotiations. It will take more than an executive mandate to create this cooperative environment between the project team, business owners, and end-users.

Building momentum

One of the known disadvantages with a traditional big bang deployment approach is that business value generation (i.e., software in production) is slow. People naturally like to be identified with successful implementation projects and stay away from projects that are not going anywhere. When a project gains momentum, then it is harder to derail the effort.

The project team does not need to build momentum and excitement **after** the implementation project but **during** the project! The best method to accomplish this is to generate quick wins early in the project. The result has be something tangible and that generates some level of value to the customer. It could be building a proof of concept that demonstrates that the packaged software will support the customer's business. It could be an implementation of the business software for a strategic department or region. It could be an implementation of the basic functionality of the packaged software. Whatever the project team determines as the quick win, it must meet the following objectives:

1. The result demonstrates that the packaged business software can competently support the business.

2. The result demonstrates that the project team can deliver a business solution for the organization.

3. The result is perceived as valuable by key stakeholders.

4. The project team can build upon the initial result.

5. The result generates excitement and organizational adoption.

Point #1: Customers gain confidence with packaged software based on how the software performs during a sales demonstration. That confidence grows exponentially when customers witness how the packaged software performs with their own data in their own environment. With that growth in confidence comes growth in support and trust.

Point #2: The chances are that this implementation is the first time that the project team (Business, IT, Implementation Partner) has come together to implement packaged software. Just as you need to build confidence outside the project team, you also need to build confidence inside the project team. No challenge is too big for confident and committed people.

Point #3: The project team has to deliver a result that is deemed valuable by the key stakeholders. The odds are that a completed requirements specification document is not perceived as a huge value generator to a business owner. Key stakeholders see working software as valuable. But herein lies the trap. In general, packaged software is logically built and designed to integrate with other software. There are technical dependencies that dictate the sequence in which the packaged software is configured and implemented. Certain packaged software features may depend on other features being implemented as well. In situations where these dependencies are not well documented, the project team will naturally gravitate towards a big bang approach to reduce implementation risk. In order to be able to create these quick wins, the implementation partner must understand the documented and undocumented technical dependencies in order to carve out a feature set that can be implemented quickly.

 Challenge to implementation partners

Carving out a subset of software features can be a challenge given the dependencies inherent in packaged software. However, by providing guidance on packaged software feature scope, you enable the customer to take a more iterative, risk-adverse approach with their implementation. You also help the customers to realize the value from their software investment sooner rather than later. For customers, if the implementation partners cannot provide you with this guidance, then this would raise a question regarding how well the implementation partner knows the COTS software.

Point #4: The project team agrees upon a result, but this result has to be one that can be expanded upon. The result must empower the project team to make decisions faster and be better focused on the end solution.

Point #5: The result has to be something that is visible and has a measurable impact. Implementing a set of back-office (i.e., administrative, not customer facing) features may be necessary but by itself will not have a huge impact. A customer of mine said it well, "We need to balance 'Give them what they want' with 'Give them what they need'" to generate real adoption and excitement.

Building project momentum through early successes is a key tactic for developing trust between the negotiating parties. When the decision to select packaged software is communicated to the customer's organization, then stakeholders' current perceptions of packaged software will initially drive expectations. What is required is a marketing effort to align perceptions to focus on the inherent advantages of packaged software.

Marketing your solution

Marketing is all about managing and developing perceptions. The perceptions that your stakeholders and end users have regarding the proposed business solution is the reality that the project team has to manage. The project team has to make the effort to ensure that their business solution is seen and positioned in the best possible light. Historically, this has been addressed through a project communication plan, yet communications plans typically focus on building perceptions and not changing perceptions.

Knowledge is power, and power is personal. Implementing packaged software will result in a shift in knowledge and power. This change can be perceived as a personal threat. Given this perceived negative impact, it is important that the project team balance this impact with the opportunities and positive impact associated with a new business solution. Historically, project communication plans have only dealt with the negative impact of a business solution implementation. The project team needs to ensure that a balanced message that fosters adoption and excitement is communicated!

Effective marketing of your business solution to project stakeholders will include the following areas:

1. **Highlight your business solution's advantages**. When change is communicated, people can easily identify the negative impacts to them personally. Make sure that there is a balanced message between the impacts and benefits of a new business solution.

2. **Establish a project image/logo**. A picture is worth a thousand words. While I concede that a project image/logo is not the best use of effort for a small midsize company—it is something to consider for larger companies that are matrixed and have a sensitive political landscape. Image counts when it comes to advertising and promoting your business solution.

3. **Don't try to be everything to everyone**. No business solution will appeal to everyone. Adoption will never be 100%. Focus on the key stakeholders and the user groups that will have the greatest impact on your business solution's success.

4. **Monitor your marketing/advertising**. Is the project team effective in setting expectations for the project? How is the project being perceived by the organization? Are you building trust or confusion? Most implementations spend more effort on communicating and less effort on listening to see if adoption is taking root.

An effective marking strategy is based upon the realization that the project team will have to negotiate with their stakeholders to foster effective adoption and support. Just as your packaged software partner had to sell their solution to the customer, now the project team needs to position and sell their solution to the internal organization. Nothing encourages acceptance more than success.

Summary

Packaged software functionality will never exactly meet the customer's existing software expectations. Packaged software is designed to meet a broad set of common business requirements for a particular market or industry. [2] While tradeoffs are common in any "software" engineering endeavor, tradeoffs in this case are driven by the desire to leverage components from the marketplace. This is a change in philosophy that not only the project team must make, but also stakeholders and end users, if real adoption and acceptance is to be obtained.

Successful packaged software implementations are those implementations that are able to balance tradeoffs, resulting in minimizing the Total Cost of Ownership and maximizing organizational acceptance. The first step in finding this balance is to understand when to negotiate on business requirements. The second step is to lay the groundwork for effective negotiations. This effort includes sending a balanced message (impacts, opportunities) along with setting appropriate expectations (achievable goals) for the new business solution. Throughout this effort, the stakeholders and end users must view the project team as trusted advisors. Trust is something that is earned and there is no better way to earn trust than by focusing on quick wins. Quick wins build momentum, organizational support, acceptance, and confidence. Confidence will enable the project team to lead the organization in the implementation of a business solution. The next chapter will define a new project role that will increase the chance for success with packaged software.

References

1. Panorama Consulting, *2008 ERP Report – Part 1*, Panorama Consulting, 2008, Page 1.

2. Albert & Brownsword., *Evolutionary Process for Integrating COTS-Based Systems (EPIC)*, Software Engineering Institute, 2002, Section A, Page 15.

10
Have a Business Solution Architect

We must deal with the realities of requirements and configuration conflicts.

In today's environment, the majority of customers have a functional organizational structure where personnel are grouped by functional specialty, (example: sales, operations, human resources). This structure works well for division of effort and specialization. However, it does create challenges when managing business processes and the systems that support them. It is rare to see a business process that is completely supported by only one functional area. A functional requirement can add value to an individual group or function but can also have a negative impact across the business process/solution. A traditional packaged software implementation approach based upon functional silos will not identify these negative impacts until the testing phase at the end of an implementation. At this point, there are very few options available, and these negative impacts are usually addressed in a triage manner that results in a greater Total Cost of Ownership for the customer.

What is required is a new project team role that will address both requirements and packaged software configuration conflicts. This new role will search for and identify these conflicts early in the implementation, so that the project team can effectively address them. To actively find conflicts, the project team needs to first understand where potential conflicts can occur. Business requirements conflicts occur at the conceptual level (independent of software), whereas configuration conflicts occur at the physical level (within the software). The next section further describes how the key players in a packaged software implementation will view a business solution model.

Perspectives of a Business solution

How can the project team see potential conflicts up-front and address them early in the implementation process? It starts with being able to view a business solution from both a conceptual and a physical perspective. Let's review the conceptual and physical perspectives of a business solution.

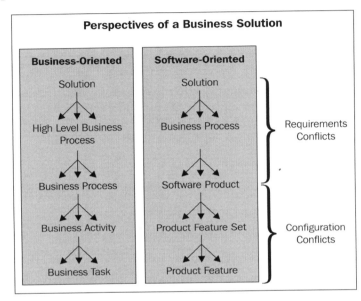

Each of the key players (Business, IT, Implementation Partner) in a COTS implementation may view the business solution differently. Business owners and end users will tend to view a solution from a business perspective. Technology-oriented players like IT and the Implementation Partner will tend to view a solution from a software perspective. There are five levels used to define a business solution (solution, business process, software product, product feature set, product feature). What is important to note is that business requirements conflicts occur at the conceptual level (independent of software), whereas configuration conflicts happen at the physical level (software dependent).

Case Study

I will elaborate on the above model by way of a real-life example. I had the opportunity to lead an implementation of a packaged project accounting solution for a Fortune 100 company. As part of the implementation, our project team worked on developing a new solution model. There were two competing views of the business solution. One was a view of the business solution that focused strictly on the business activities that needed to be performed, independent of the software. Then, there was another view of the business solution that focused on how the business activities were supported by technology. As part of this process to create the new solution model, I made the following observations:

1. Both views are required and support different objectives. One view is not superior nor can replace the other.

2. It is important to see the separation between the conceptual (i.e., what business activities to perform) and the physical (i.e., how the software supports the business activities). Too often, we want to go straight to an answer before we fully define the question. Having this separation also enabled the project team to focus on the appropriate area for problem solving (i.e., is this a business process issue or a software issue?).

3. Conflicts happen both at the conceptual (requirements) and physical (configuration) levels.

Referring back to the above illustration, we will note that focus at the business process level is important in identifying both potential requirements conflicts and configuration conflicts.

Who is covering business processes?

Traditional packaged software implementation approaches would try to cover all five levels of the solution by the following roles:

- Project manager
- Functional lead
- Architect lead
- Technical lead

The project manager and the functional lead(s) have to be able to represent, evaluate, and communicate across all five levels (i.e., solution, business process, software product, product feature set, product feature) concurrently. This is quite a load to carry by two roles whose primary function is to focus and operate below the business process level. The technical lead and architect lead focus on the technology infrastructure across the business solution. These roles might address the technology conflicts but may not be totally effective in identifying business functional requirements and configuration conflicts. Also, consider the natural tendencies to become only focused on one's individual task assignments and responsibilities during the implementation.

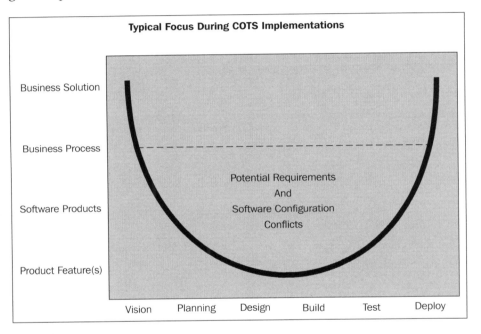

As we move through the early strategy phases (**Vision, Planning**) into the construction phases (**Design, Build**), the project team will naturally refine their focus on accomplishing the implementation tasks. These implementation tasks tend to be more function-oriented and not business process-oriented. Using a traditional waterfall model, the validation at the business process and solution levels does not occur until the end of the implementation cycle. This effect is the key reason for having an iterative approach in order to compress the time cycle and provide an opportunity for validation at the higher levels during the earlier implementation phases.

In addition to the above recommendation, another best implementation practice is having a project team role that is dedicated to focusing at the business process level. A business solution architect is a role that can enable your project team to identify business requirements and software configuration conflicts early in the implementation cycle. This new implementation role can be filled by an existing functional lead with a broad knowledge across a business process, or could be a dedicated individual, depending on the project size and scope.

Solution - Business Solution Architect

A business solution architect is a functional resource that has the ability to participate across all of the functional areas of a business solution. An implementation partner should provide a business solution architect who has participated in several implementations of the targeted business solution. The business solution architect should have an understanding of both the business process and how the packaged software supports the business process. Most important is that a business solution architect must be someone who is able to lead and persuade others in their recommendations because they will have a huge impact on customer decisions.

Responsibilities

Key responsibilities for the business solution architect include:

- Identifying and addressing conflicting business requirements
- Identifying and addressing conflicting packaged software configuration decisions
- Performing knowledge transfer with the customer in order to build a business solution architect capability internally
- Defining a business process management framework for the customer to leverage moving forward

As with any implementation, when the project team refines their focus on execution, there is a tendency to fixate only on a functional silo and lose focus on the business process. This is where the business solution architect operates. This responsibility applies to both requirements and software configurations. The business solution architect can support and assist the functional leads in gathering requirements and software configuration as long it does not prohibit the business solution architect from keeping focus on the entire business process.

The business solution architect is not just a role required during the implementation, but is also required after the implementation, when the customer plans to change their packaged software configuration. As the customer considers opportunities to add new functionality or address business process improvements, the business solution architect plays a key role in helping to find the right approach across the business solution. Conducting a knowledge transfer will enable the customer to support their new business solution. Along the same lines of customer enablement, the business solution architect should work with the customer to define a business process management framework that enables the customer to quickly realize greater business value from their investment.

As the role of a business solution architect is not a standard role defined by implementation partners, the next section addresses the qualifications for this role.

Qualifications

A business solution architect is an individual who has the following capabilities:

- Understands the business model (40%)
- Understands the product functionality (40%)
- Understands the supporting technical infrastructure (20%)

A business solution architect is an individual who is able to understand and appreciate the key areas involved in the business solution implementation. Understanding the business is a key priority for the business solution architect. If one does not understand the business, then how can one lead or persuade a customer on the correct requirements selection and software configuration approach. There will be situations where the business solution architect will act as a resource for the other project team members—especially when business involvement is limited due to time constraints and other responsibilities. Business solution architects do not need to know every aspect of the packaged software project's functionality and capabilities, but they do need to know the key software features that support the business process critical path or main success scenario. Finally, any individual in the role of an architect should have a holistic understanding of the technology that is supporting the business solution. It's less about having a deep knowledge in a specific area, and more about having a broad knowledge across all aspects of the business solution. Having a business solution architect will benefit the project team in several ways, but the most important is in the area of business requirements conflict. To identify these conflicts early, it is important to know where to look.

Best practices for identifying conflicts

When it comes to requirements and configuration conflicts, it is important to take a practical approach. It is not a question of *if* these conflicts will occur but rather *when* these conflicts will occur. Identifying requirements and software configuration conflicts early in the implementation will enable the project team to effectively deal with these challenges.

Identify functional boundaries

Identifying the functional boundaries within a business process is a key requirement for highlighting potential business requirement conflicts. Handoffs between organizations provide real insight into whether business activities are executed at the same level of proficiency across the business process. If the levels of execution or proficiency are different, then it may be a sign that the underlying business requirements may be based upon different levels of maturity. Different levels of maturity are a definite red flag, indicating that conflicting business requirement may exist. If this occurs, then the project team should lead the customer in making decisions that best support business results – not individual business functions.

Identify packaged software dependencies and shared components

Packaged software is designed to be logical and integrated. Just as a business model has assumptions and constraints that support the model, packaged business software has technical assumptions and constraints that support the underlying logical data model. This results in software functionality relying on other software functionality being present, and software configurations supporting other downstream software configurations. It is important to know and understand these technical assumptions and constraints up-front, so that the decisions made take into consideration these software dependencies.

Packaged business software also uses the concept of shared components (data) that support product features across multiple business processes. For example, vendor information can be used in procurement, supply chain, and human resource business processes. Each business process can have different requirements for vendor information, which may be in conflict with one another. This is another example of where negotiation needs to occur between the different stakeholders.

Challenge for implementation partners

As part of the configuration for packaged business software, implementation partners should provide a configuration workbook to assist the customer in making configuration decisions. At a minimum, the configuration workbook should provide the following:

- Prioritized sequence of packaged software configuration set-up steps. Some configuration components (i.e., list of customer types) must be defined before other components (i.e., list of customers) can be established.

- Configuration considerations for each configuration component. What are the questions that the customer needs to address before making a decision on values for a specific configuration table?

- Software dependencies for each configuration component. What are the dependencies and impacts that each configuration table has across the packaged software?

- Shared data components across the packaged software. Consider having requirements and design sessions for these shared data components across all of the supported business areas.

Providing this level of guidance will enable implementation partners to proactively identify potential software configuration conflicts.

Perform a business process-oriented review of requirements and software configuration

The project team, you should review the business requirements and software configurations in totality. A holistic review of business requirements is typically done as part of a formal Fit/Gap session. Unfortunately, software configuration reviews are less structured and are typically performed on an individual functional basis. This approach is becoming more the standard because the project team is in build mode and it's hard to bring people back up to a solution level when they are digging the trenches. Having a business solution architect role on your project team will help reduce the risk of software configuration conflicts.

Validate conflicts

I have never met an individual who could completely identify all of the potential conflicts across business requirements and packaged software configurations. Business solution modeling is the best method of validating the conflicts that exist. A strategic advantage in implementing packaged software is that you have working software early in the implementation cycle. Take full advantage of this capability to validate assumptions, constraints, dependencies, and decisions.

Assign work in a process-oriented fashion

In today's ever-increasing competitive environment, we are being asked to implement COTS software faster. Project managers use a work breakdown structure to identify the tasks and the resulting deliverables required to meet project objectives. Project managers then assign resources (i.e., team members) to perform the tasks and complete the deliverables. Two popular project management approaches for reducing the implementation timeframe are **crashing** and **fast tracking**. Simply put, crashing is adding resources to the implementation in order to do more in less time. On the other hand, fast tracking is about doing activities in parallel. Both approaches are undesirable for the following reasons:

- Crashing requires a further breakdown of implementation activities into smaller functional activities. As the project team break down work into smaller units, the greater the probability of tunnel vision and losing sight of the big picture.

- Fast tracking limits team member's exposure to related/dependent areas because the project team are doing more activities in parallel.

Too often, we assign work in our implementation project plans based upon a functional breakdown structure and not a business process breakdown structure. If the work breakdown structure is functional, then eventually, our project team will only think functionally. In order to identify conflicts across a business solution, we must first have the appropriate view during the implementation. Having a business process oriented project work breakdown structure will support the appropriate view. Following are guidelines to follow in creating a business process-oriented project plan:

- Project team members are assigned to business processes, not to an individual packaged software product

- Business process dependencies are identified and incorporated into the project's work breakdown structure

Following is a comparison and contrast of a functional-oriented project plan and a business process-oriented project plan.

Functional vs Business Process Project Plan

Functional-Oriented WBS		Business-Oriented WBS	
WBS ID	**Activity Name**	**WBS ID**	**Activity Name**
1	Vision	1	Vision
2	Planning	2	Planning
3	Design	3	Design
3.1	Procurement	3.1	Procure to Pay business process
3.2	Purchasing	3.2	Supply Chain business process
3.3	Accounts Payable		
3.4	Manufacturing		
3.5	Engineering		
3.6	Inventory		

Even if you are only implementing one packaged software product (e.g., purchasing) within a single business process (e.g., procure to pay) the project team must look across the entire business process to ensure that the desired business results are created. Too often, we limit packaged software implementation scope to only the COTS software we are implementing and do not consider the larger business process scope. Excluding the appropriate business process scope increases the possibility of conflicts with existing legacy systems.

Summary

It is not a possibility that requirements and software configuration conflicts may arise, but rather it is a reality that these conflicts will arise. As the project team progresses in the business solution implementation, they will run against conflicts—both from a business and from a technology perspective. The best approach is to quickly identify these types of conflicts early, so that the project team has the time to correctly deal with these conflicts across the business solution.

To proactively identify requirements and software configuration conflicts, the project team needs to have the correct role for the job. Having a business solution architect in the lead will enable the implementation to focus across all levels of a business solution, in order to identify conflicts. These conflicts usually arise from functional focus that naturally occurs in business and during the implementation. If we look from a knowledge transfer perspective, we would agree that a single project role will provide the most value to the customer. A customer should provide an internal resource to closely partner with the implementation partner's business solution architect.

Business requirements and software configuration conflicts are known risks for packaged software implementations, which can have a significant impact on a project's success. Therefore, it is important that the project team takes an iterative, risk-averse approach to addressing these areas.

1. First, identify the areas for potential business requirement conflicts, such as functional boundaries.

2. Second, work with the implementation partner to determine the assumptions, constraints, and dependencies inherent with the packaged software.

3. Third, formally review the business requirements and software configurations across the entire business solution.

4. Fourth, conduct business solution modeling to validate conflicts.

The more chances the project team to be successful, the greater the chances are of being successful. However, without the appropriate knowledge, one can have all the chances in the world and still miss the mark. In our final chapter, we will focus on effective knowledge generation.

11

Accelerate Decisions by Generating More Knowledge and Less Information

Decisions drive implementations!

I grew up in a time where information was hard to come by. Generating information was seen as a valuable exercise because information was so limited. The first software development methodology I learned was the Waterfall model. One of the key focus areas for Waterfall was documentation. However, there was a limit to what value documentation/information could provide. In our enthusiasm to create information, we actually went down to an extreme where too much project information was becoming a roadblock.

 Case Study

I briefly participated in a project for a packaged software implementation where the project team were using a variation of the Waterfall methodology for the implementation approach. The project scope was for a single business process (IT portfolio management). The project was one year behind schedule and around 1.5 million dollars over budget. I was asked to participate in a business design session for a business activity that was in scope for the project I was leading. Nothing unusual at first until this one individual announced himself as the "requirements guru".

This peaked my curiosity, so I asked more specifics about the role. His role was to scroll through the 200-page requirements document during project meetings to ensure that existing business requirements were neither duplicated nor compromised. I asked if anyone else on the project team had read the entire requirements document and he said no—that's why his role existed. As I watched the meeting unfold, I saw discussions suspended as everyone waited for the "requirements guru" to do a search on the requirements document to find potential issues. Needless to say, there were more action items and fewer decisions made during the session. This is a prime example of where documentation/information became more of a roadblock and less of a decision enabler.

From a project management perspective, I have noted where project team members excel in producing documentation and focus less on producing decisions. Producing documentation is far easier than producing decision(s)). As implementation partners, we have created this false sense of accomplishment by measuring how much documentation we produce. We have this false perception that generating more documentation will result in more knowledge and greater decision-making capabilities. Nothing is further from the truth. In fact, too much non-value-added data mixed in with the value-added data will result in confusion, frustration, and people avoiding documentation all together. The documentation that the project team produces is reflective of the information gathering approach that is utilized. Before eliminating non-value-added documentation, we must first look at how the project team gathers information.

Traditional information gathering approach

The traditional method for gathering information as part of a packaged software implementation was to take an exploratory approach. This method relied on open-ended questions that resulted in generating the maximum amount of information. The project team would analyze this data in order to identify what information would be useful. There are challenges associated with an exploratory approach:

1. Additional effort is required by the project team to review and analyze a larger volume of information in order to determine the relevance to the implementation.
2. Waste of effort in gathering non-value-added information.
3. May create confusion or inappropriate expectations by gathering information pertaining to a business area considered out of scope for the implementation.

An exploratory method of information gathering is useful early in the implementation where the project objectives and scope have not been defined. However, once the project charter has been clearly stated, the project team should focus on only gathering information that will help to generate the appropriate knowledge to support decision-makers.

Information versus knowledge

Is there a difference between information and knowledge? Absolutely! I view knowledge as a simple equation:

Information + Inference = Knowledge

Information must be available before knowledge can be generated. However, information by itself does not generate knowledge. It supports knowledge generation. Knowledge is generated only when an individual uses inference (i.e., their brain) to interpret information appropriately. Inference is how people draw conclusions. Producing a great volume of documentation does not result in producing a great amount of knowledge. In fact, it has been my experience that personal interactions generate a greater volume of knowledge than documentation.

I have been involved in implementation projects where a tremendous amount of effort was spent on gathering information that produced a small amount of relevant knowledge. To maximize the knowledge we can generate, we have to be smart and purposeful about the information that we produce. Gathering the information is half the battle. Knowledge is a human trait and not a technology trait. We also must present information in such a manner (context) that facilitates knowledge generation and making decisions.

Knowledge is the ability to apply information gathered to perform a business result (decision). When the **right information** is communicated in the **right context**, the greater the **knowledge created**, and the **faster** key **decisions** are made. Information gathering takes on a whole new light when seen from the perspective of driving decisions.

Decision-oriented information gathering

I will now share an approach that I've used to accelerate decision-making and thus accelerate implementations. It is a method that first considers the decisions that must be made and then gathers the appropriate information required by the decision makers. The first step is to define what decisions must be made.

Implementation scope defines the decisions

Before the project team begins information gathering, they must first consider what decisions the project needs to make. The implementation scope for a packaged software implementation is what we need to begin. Consider the following illustration:

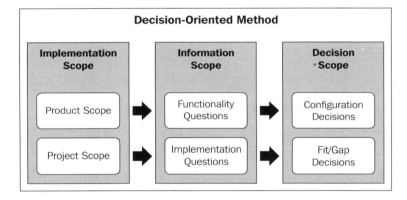

Simply stated, the scope for a packaged software implementation consists of the software features that will be deployed (product scope) and the project activities and audience for the deployment (project scope). Once the implementation scope has been defined, the project team can better define the information requirements and key decisions that must be made. There are two types of information requirements for a COTS implementation—one type that deals with the targeted functionality to be deployed and the other type that focuses on the specific project activities to perform. Gathering the required information and presenting it in the appropriate context will enable the project team to make both software configuration and fit/gap decisions.

Challenge for implementation partners

Implementation partners should provide sets of predefined functionality and implementation questionnaires to assist in gathering information. These questionnaires should be progressively elaborate— meaning that there should be a logical progression in the questions to a deeper focus on a specific area. The questionnaires should also be grouped in a manner that allows sets of questions to be eliminated based upon the packaged software implementation scope.

An implementation partner may not know every single decision that the customer must make as part of their packaged software implementation, but implementation partners should be able to identify up-front the key decisions required, based upon the implementation scope. In the next section, we will discuss how best practices can have an impact on accelerating decisions.

Best practices influence the decisions

A best practice is a process, method, or approach that is considered the most effective at delivering a desired outcome. A best practice is repeatable and has proven itself over a period of time. For COTS implementations, there are two areas of best practice that should be considered:

1. Industry best practices

2. Configuration best practices

We will revisit our previous illustration to determine where to best utilize industry and configuration best practices.

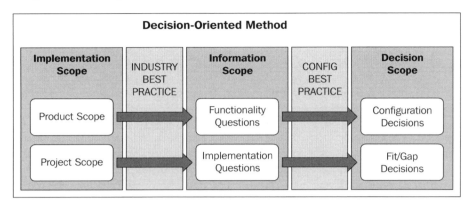

Once the implementation scope has been clearly defined, industry best practices should be leveraged by the project team to assist the customer in answering questions. Providing these best practices up-front to the customer will streamline information gathering. As the project team moves from gathering information to driving decisions on packaged software configuration and Fit/Gap, configuration and gap decision best practices can be referenced in order to provide proven knowledge to key decision makers.

 ### Challenge for implementation partners

Implementation partners should be able to provide industry, implementation, and configuration best practices to their customers. These best practices should be formally documented and provided early in the implementation, where they have the greatest benefit. These documents will provide evidence that the implementation partner can provide a repeatable and reliable service.

Gathering information is an important first step in making decisions. In the next section, we will describe the process of using this gathered information to develop the knowledge required for effective decision-making.

Effective knowledge generation

Effective knowledge generation first starts with gathering the right information. It also means leveraging multiple channels in order to gather information. In the case of defining business requirements, information gathering should be an iterative process where each iteration refines the scope of your investigation (discovery). For supporting effective knowledge generation, we need to perform the following tasks:

- Gather
- Review
- Refine
- Relate

Gather information

First, your information gathering approach should be in alignment with the implementation scope. Asking questions outside the area of interest is a waste of time and effort, and may cause confusion for the customer. Second, in order to understand the information that you receive, you need to understand the context of that information. A suggested approach to gathering information is to start at the business solution level and then drill down into the existing components that support the business solution.

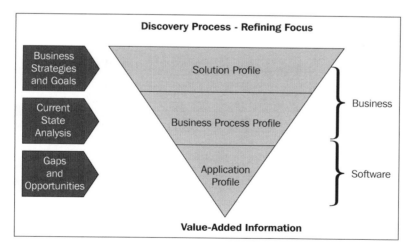

To effectively gather the complete set of information required to generate sufficient knowledge, the project team must start with business objectives and progressively elaborate the objectives until they reach the supporting structures (i.e., processes, people, software). The project team should structure information gathering in such a manner as to only focus on the critical information requirements, while quickly removing discovery areas that are not relevant.

For example, consider a packaged software functionality questionnaire. This type of document is typically used by implementation partners to gather additional information required for scoping a COTS implementation project. However, on more than one occasion, I have seen cases where the question sequence provided in the document was based upon the order of software configuration, not the order of business execution. This created an inconsistent experience for the customer, and created subtle conflicts in the implementation scope—the customer could not determine what their focus should be. The project team sets expectations based upon the questions they ask. Based upon my experience and lessons learned, the following are best practices for gathering information from customers:

- Sequence questions in such a way as to educate the customer in the software and business solution that is the focus. I have experienced great success by using the "day in the life" approach to sequence questions across the business solution.

- Tier questions to further understand/gather specific information requirements (i.e., Level 1, Level 2 questionnaires). This method will enable the project team to quickly eliminate questions that are not relevant to the implementation scope.

- There should be more questions on the business than on the software. Only when you understand the business model (conceptual) can you effectively delve into the specific software-related questions (physical).

Now for a brief illustration of the concepts above:

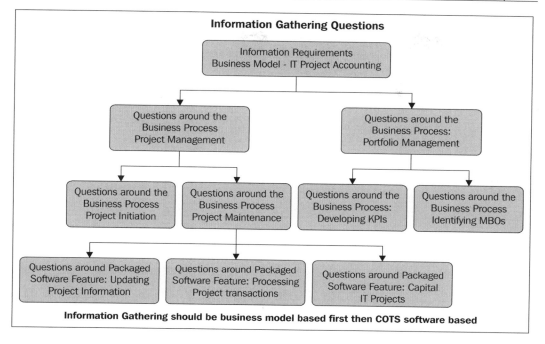

Information Gathering Questions

Information Requirements
Business Model - IT Project Accounting

Questions around the
Business Process
Project Management

Questions around the
Business Process:
Portfolio Management

Questions around the
Business Process
Project Initiation

Questions around the
Business Process
Project Maintenance

Questions around the
Business Process:
Developing KPIs

Questions around the
Business Process
Identifying MBOs

Questions around Packaged
Software Feature: Updating
Project Information

Questions around Packaged
Software Feature: Processing
Project transactions

Questions around Packaged
Software Feature: Capital
IT Projects

Information Gathering should be business model based first then COTS software based

Key points to note:

- Information gathering is based upon the business model, not the products. As with most packaged or COTS software products, business processes will span multiple software products. I believe that one of the main challenges with integration is that information is gathered in silos based upon software product boundaries.

- An implementation partner can make the update process more manageable by segregating out the different levels of implementation questions. A challenge for any implementation partner is updating implementation questions as new packaged software releases are created. However, it is interesting to note that some sets of questions (software -specific) change more frequently than other sets (business -specific).

Once the project team has gathered the information, the next step is to evaluate the information to determine how to best use it in generating knowledge.

Review information (evaluate)

As the project team gathers data during the implementation, the team need a process for evaluating the data in order to access the knowledge generation potential. The first step in this process is to review the information that the project team have gathered in order to determine what information is relevant versus what information is supplemental. To maximize the efforts, the project team want to focus on the information that will help the customer drive to the decisions they need to make as part of the implementation.

Refining information (enrich)

Once the project team have identified the information that will have a direct impact on making decisions, the next step is to refine the information gathered. This is where an implementation partner can add tremendous value. The right implementation partner can enrich information gathered, by leveraging the following:

1. Benchmark data from industry leaders.
2. Intellectual capital from other implementations.

Simply to transcribe a meeting and putting the meeting notes on a project team server is not enough. One of the key values an implementation partner can provide is sharing experiences and information gathered from similar business solution implementations.

Relate information (context)

The final step in preparing information for effective knowledge generation is connecting the various pieces of information into a complete picture for a specific area. Too often this exercise is not performed and the customer has to piece the information together themselves. This typically results in confusion and the information not being referenced because too much effort is required to bring the disjointed information into the appropriate context. Only when the information is brought into the correct context can the information be used to generate knowledge. The best practice for bringing information into context is to group it into a logical order based upon a business process or a "day in the life" for a business role. Relating information to what the customer knows today makes it easier for the customer to assimilate new information into their knowledgebase (i.e. brains).

When decision-makers have the correct knowledge, they can make informed decisions quickly. Having the correct knowledge begins with gathering the correct information. As the information is gathered, the project team reviews, refines, and connects these pieces ofinformation together, in order to convey a compelling story for decision-makers.

This far, in this chapter, we have been dealing with the input to decision-makers. Now, we need to focus on the decision-makers themselves. The project team needs to prepare decision-makers to make decisions when the time comes.

Enabling decision makers

It has been my experience that decision-makers will not make a decision until they have some level of confidence in the outcome, and they are comfortable with making the decision. One criteria is objective, and the other criterion is subjective. I have found that when decision-makers have a competent understanding of the packaged software implementation, they are more comfortable in making decisions. The following sections will focus on best practices for building a competent understanding for decision-makers.

Project on-boarding

A reality in any packaged software implementation is that decision-makers will come and go during the implementation. The challenge is to be able to quickly bring in new decision-makers without a major disruption to the overall project momentum. The traditional approach is to create documentation to a level such that anyone can review it independently, in order to integrate themselves into the project. This documentation style is overkill and is not the most effective use of project resources. It is a futile attempt because documentation by itself is never successful in bringing new people up to speed. There are always tacit knowledge and conversations that are never documented. The primary audience for project documentation is the project team—not individuals outside of the project. The best approach is to have a project on-boarding process. The goal of this is to provide the appropriate level of information and project background before allowing the individual to participate and make decisions.

Also, this approach provides the project team the opportunity to understand the value the individual would bring to the team. I've had situations where individuals (including business executives) wanted to be involved solely for the sake of being in the communication chain and expanding their influence. This is human nature, and I have done the same myself. Understanding the value that an individual can bring to the project will help the project team understand how best to leverage the individual in the implementation project. Having a formal project on-boarding process acts as filter to ensure that the project team maintain project momentum. It is far easier to make a decision with four people than with forty people. The key is to find the four people that have the most organizational influence and that can persuade others to accept the decisions that they have made.

Maximize interactions with the project team

Comfort and trust are related. If decision-makers have trust in the project team then they will be in a better position to make decisions quickly. Interaction is key in building trust. Interaction is also a vital way of sharing information and knowledge at a more personal level. The project team should not simply rely on documentation to generate knowledge for decision-makers.

Summary

Gathering information is an important step in conducting a business solution implementation—especially in order to understand the customer's current environment. Information is the first step in generating the knowledge required to make informed decisions. However, information alone does not guarantee that knowledge is created quickly. It is important that we enrich and relate the information that facilitates accelerated knowledge generation. Knowledge will drive the key decisions that the project team needs to make during the implementation.

A critical discipline necessary for an implementation is knowledge management. At a very high level, knowledge management is about managing the intellectual capital that helps an organization or team to make decisions. And it is fair to say that there are plenty of decisions to be made during a business solution implementation. Therefore, it makes sense that we understand how to leverage the lessons of knowledge management in order to assist the project team in managing and leveraging the information generated during an implementation. In the final chapter, we will revisit the principles expanded upon in this book and discuss how to evolve our strategy for implementing packaged software.

12
Changing the Game

No problem can be solved from the same level of consciousness that created it. - Albert Einstein.

Today, more customers are moving to packaged or Commercial Off The Shelf (COTS) software to support their enterprise business processes. COTS software offers several potential advantages over the traditional approach of developing business software internally:

- Rapid delivery to business
- Sharing development costs with the external software provider
- Standardization across the enterprise
- Effective use of the customer's limited technology resources
- Allows greater focus on strategic processes

Many customers have learned that the above are only **potential** advantages of packaged software. There is no guarantee that the customer will realize these benefits without having the correct implementation approach. For many customers, software development is not a strategic, revenue-generating activity. Customers are looking more to packaged software as a means of reducing costs. However, the majority of COTS implementations fail to provide this value due to the implementation approach taken. It is an implementation approach that focuses more on developing highly-customized solutions, which leave customers with an inflexible business solution. What is required to reverse this trend is an evolution in the implementation approach—a change that will maximize the packaged software investment and appropriately leverage all of the components of a business solution (People, Processes, and Technology).

Traditional approaches fall short

Realizing value from packaged software is determined by two key factors: software quality and the implementation approach used. In this book we have focused on the implementation approach. Enterprise Resource Planning (ERP) makes up the majority of the packaged software industry today. Let's revisit a comment made about ERP implementations:

> *Nearly 90% of ERP implementations are late or over budget and ERP implementation success rate is only about 33%* [1]

What are the reasons for such dismal performance? Some of it has to do with software quality and limitations, but the majority of the problems have to do with the implementation approach: an implementation approach that focused more on building custom solutions than maximizing the advantages of COTS software. The result was unrealized business results along with a healthy dose of cynicism.

Understanding packaged software advantages and challenges

Reversing the trend and cynicism requires a radical change in how we conduct packaged software implementations. The first step we need to take is to have an implementation strategy that maximizes the advantages of COTS software and minimize the challenges associated with implementing COTS software. Consider the following illustration:

Implementing COTS Software	
Advantages • Drive standardization across the enterprise resulting in greater operational efficiencies • Enables greater focus on strategic activities • Potential for rapid deployment of technology • Shared IT development costs • Simplify IT technical footprint	**Challenges** • Organizational change impact • Perception of setbacks • Discipline to maximize COTS software investment • Different implementation approach (solution driven vs. requirements driven)

The following sections highlight packaged software advantages and challenges that the project team should address as part of the implementation strategy.

Maximize the advantages of packaged software

The following is a list of the key advantages of packaged software. These advantages can only be realized if the project team has the correct implementation strategy.

Drive standardization

Probably the greatest value that packaged software provides is that it that supports standard business processes. Standardizing business processes can be a challenging endeavor; however, the process can be easier with the right COTS software provider. There will always be variations to the standard business process supported by the packaged software. The project team should address business process variations separately and not develop a solution based upon exceptions.

Greater focus on strategic activities

In theory, packaged software requires less customer resources to install, develop, implement, and maintain than "build from scratch" software. I use the term "in theory" because I have observed cases where the COTS software required more customer resources than the legacy software it replaced. What's important the project team to remember is that they must develop a solution that should require fewer resources to manage.

Potential for rapid deployment

This advantage is important for both existing and new functionality within the customer's organization. The single most important factor that drives this advantage is the ability to upgrade quickly and take advantage of new packaged software functionality. The second factor is almost as important, and it is the ability to quickly train and enable end-users to utilize new functionality. Organizational change management and end-user training are key strategic competencies that the customer must master in order to enable rapid deployment. From an implementation strategy perspective, the project team should lead with delivered packaged software functionality and minimize software changes. The project team should also ensure that adequate resources (i.e., tools, change agents) are used for organizational change management.

Shared IT development costs

Partnering with a viable and competent packaged software partner allows the customer to share IT development costs for business software. However, this advantage is negated if the customer does not do two things: (1) upgrade frequently, in order to leverage new software functionality, and (2) partner with the packaged software provider on new enhancements. If the customer is not in a position to upgrade frequently, or partner on new enhancements, then the customer's IT organization would experience greater pressure to make software changes to the packaged software. Additional software changes to packaged software will increase the effort required to upgrade. The project team must ensure that the packaged software implementation will put the customer in a position to upgrade quickly.

Simplify the IT footprint

IT complexity reduces IT agility. Multiple IT technologies require dedicated resources to support these various systems. Legacy systems are more prone to proprietary technologies that make it harder to leverage IT resources across individual application systems. We are seeing the trend where packaged software is being built upon open standards, which enable greater interoperability. However, it is important to note that taking a "best of breed" approach to packaged software may result in more complexity — not less.

 Case Study

I recently had the opportunity to work with a customer on how to maximize their packaged software investment. After reviewing their current business systems environment, I observed that the customer had four COTS software applications supporting their business model. I did further investigation to understand why, and the customer said that they selected the COTS software that provided the greatest functionality. However, the customer was not able to leverage the individual packaged software functionality due to integration limitations. And therein lies the trap. Rarely is a complete business process encompassed in a single packaged software application. Software is only as good as its ability to integrate with other software that supports the other activities within a business process. The more integrated the packaged software is with the existing customer's IT environment, the more successful the packaged software will be in supporting business value generation for the customer.

Project teams implementing packaged software must make a conscious effort to maximize the potential value. This will require a mindset change not only within the core project team but also for all external stakeholders. Creating the required change starts with the correct implementation approach. The project team must also address the inherent challenges associated with packaged software. In the next section, we will highlight the key packaged software challenges that the project team should minimize as part of the implementation.

Minimize challenges with packaged software

In order to have a comprehensive strategy for packaged software, the project team must address both the advantages and challenges associated with packaged software. The following is a list of the key challenges of packaged software that the project team must address as part of their implementation strategy.

Organizational change impact

We will first revisit a couple of concepts for packaged software. First, packaged software is designed to meet common business requirements across a wide audience (marketplace, industry). Second, to gain any Return on Investment (ROI) in the short-term, and reduce Total Cost of Ownership (TCO) in the long-term, the customer's organization must make changes to better align itself with the delivered packaged software's functionality. Even as the customer moves forward with the packaged software, there will be change (i.e., upgrades). There are two strategies to deal with this challenge:

1. Build an organizational competency for change. Making software changes to packaged software simply to eliminate the organizational change is using technology as a crutch. People are the most flexible and adaptable component of a business solution.

2. Let Business (the customer) drive the change as much as possible. When people feel that technology (an outside party) is driving the change, then adoption becomes a greater challenge.

Perception of setbacks

This is not a possibility but a reality. The chances are that the customer is replacing highly-customized business software with broader, marketplace-oriented business software. Regardless of whether the change will result in less functionality, the perception is there. The key strategy for addressing this challenge is to focus on the longer term benefits associated with packaged software. Packaged software is not a short-term fix, but rather a long-term strategy.

Discipline to maximize COTS investment

This strategy is not only relevant during the implementation but also after the implementation. This philosophy cannot just be an "IT-oriented" process that filters end user requests. This approach must permeate throughout the entire organization. It must be more than a procedure or policy—education must be involved. Every user of packaged software should understand how to best leverage the investment!

Different implementation approach

If the customer's executive management has made the decision to not build a customized, software solution, then why should the project team only use an approach that focuses on building a custom software solution? Using a requirements-driven approach will identify both value-added and non-value-added requirements, which will result in a greater number of gaps. Using a solution-driven approach will encourage business users to maximize delivered packaged software functionality.

In the previous sections, we have defined what needs to be changed as part of a packaged software implementation; the next section will define how to implement these changes.

Change the game by changing strategy

What is needed is an approach that maximizes the advantages and minimizes the challenges. Packaged software is not a short-term sale, but a long-term relationship. It is a relationship that must evolve from a **vendor/customer** relationship to a **partner** relationship. Only at the partner relationship level can both parties maximize the value of packaged software.

Your focus determines your direction. To truly evolve COTS implementations, we need to concentrate on the following key strategies:

1. **Focus on business results**

    Too often, we fixate on packaged software features, not ensuring that the desired business result is achieved. The chances are that the customer's existing business model is not totally efficient (i.e., Lean) and effective (i.e., Quality). Therefore, it's fair to say that the project team will gather requirements that support non-value-added business activities and business results. The strategy here is to focus on the "critical path" requirements that support value-added business results and not waste time and effort on capturing all of the requirements and then filtering these during Fit/Gap analysis. The latter approach is reactive and is time consuming.

2. **Invest time in your implementation partners**

   Customers, your implementation partners include your internal IT organization, the outside consulting firm, and the COTS software provider. All three players need to have a competent understanding of your business model. All three players also need to hear the same message. Instead of taking the informal approach of educating partners via isolated meetings, customers should make an investment and conduct a structured overview of the business model from a solution, business process, and application perspective. Making this investment will minimize redundant questions and promote consistency.

3. **Implementation partners — enable your customers to lead during the implementation**

   Implementation partners, transition begins at project kickoff and not at the end of the go-live event. Effective knowledge transfer is an iterative process involving the following activities: Educate, Enable, Empower, and Celebrate. Each activity requires that the implementation partner to use a different leadership style.

4. **Perform business solution modeling**

   Business solution modeling involves executing business scenarios against a realistic, working instance of the packaged software. Business solution modeling is not a prototyping exercise carried out in order to gather requirements, but rather a validation exercise carried out in order to confirm business requirements, software configurations, and software constraints. The key results from business solution modeling include providing a visible proof of concept and building project team confidence.

5. **Determine the correct application of methodologies for your packaged software implementation**

   Packaged software implementations involve multiple disciplines (methodologies) including project management, software development, organizational change management, and business process management. One methodology is not an adequate replacement for another. The key strategy is to integrate these methodologies in order to maximize support for the project team.

6. **Implement to the current business process maturity level**

   COTS software can provide a wide array of technological capabilities and features beyond the customer's current technology footprint for a business process. However, technology alone does not mature a customer's business process. A risk-averse approach is to implement COTS software capabilities that align to the current business model. This approach will result in minimizing evolving business requirements.

7. Maximize enhancements and minimize customizations

Customers will always have unique, competitive business requirements. Enhancements are the packaged software changes that address competitive requirements. Customizations are packaged software changes that address a software defect, a missing best practice, or non-value-added requirements. A requirements gathering strategy should focus on capturing competitive business requirements and filtering out non-value-added requirements.

8. Negotiate for implementation success

Executive sponsorship is not a guarantee of effective organizational adoption. Packaged software is built upon business requirements across a broad customer/industry base, and not for a specific customer. Achieving desired results from packaged software requires a radical change in what your users expect from business software. Negotiation is required to generate both maximum value from the delivery packaged software's capabilities and maximum adoption on the part of the end users.

9. Have a business solution architect on the implementation team

It is rare for a single COTS software product to address an entire business process. For example, the compensate employees business process covers functional areas across human resources, benefits, compensation, time and attendance, payroll, and business intelligence. Because of this fact, the project team needs a role on your project team that can address business requirements and software configuration across multiple software products. Traditional implementation roles cannot adequately address potential conflicts across functional silos. A business solution architect can help the team fulfill this role.

10. Accelerate decisions by generating more knowledge and less information

Information alone does not generate business value. Information that is unreferenced — while interesting — is a waste. Only when information is applied to generate a result (decision) is knowledge created. Information is a key component in generating knowledge. However, it is how the project team gathers, review, refine, and relate information that has a knowledge impact, and not the amount of information gathered.

Summary

Implementing the principles outlined in this book requires a radical change in the approach to and the expectations of packaged software. In this book, I have defined ten guiding principles for implementing packaged software. These guiding principles or strategies must be applied appropriately by the project team. These concepts provide a means of sharing leading practice strategies for packaged software implementations. The goal is to maximize the customer's packaged software investment.

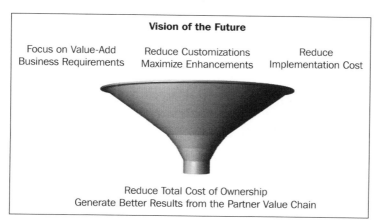

Vision of the Future

Focus on Value-Add Business Requirements   Reduce Customizations Maximize Enhancements   Reduce Implementation Cost

Reduce Total Cost of Ownership
Generate Better Results from the Partner Value Chain

Using the principles described in this book, I have been able to experience the following results:

- Reduce implementation costs by 20%.
  How?
    ○ Increase knowledge generation and sharing during the project
    ○ Reduce non-value-added documentation. Maximize interactions

- Reduce customizations by 45%.
  How?
  - Hybrid of solution-driven and requirements-driven approach
  - Maximize enhancements and Minimize customizations

- Accelerate packaged software implementations by 30%.
  How?
  - Implement to the current business process maturity level
  - Minimize evolving business requirements

- Increase ROI by 25%.
  How?
  - Upgrade in months, instead of years, by limiting packaged software changes
  - Partner with packaged software partners to incorporate enhancements into base products

These results have less to do with the packaged software and more to do with the implementation approach. Transitioning to this COTS-friendly implementation approach and strategy is an iterative process. The first step must begin with having a business solution perspective and deciding how to best leverage each component. Next, is the development of a strategy for best utilizing the packaged business software. This strategy must address the inherent advantages as well as challenges associated with COTS software. The packaged software strategy should also address the key relationships that the customer needs to develop with the implementation partner(s) and the packaged software vendor. Third and most important, business software expectations need to be redefined if packaged business software is part of the overall business solution. If business users expect a turn-key solution, then you already face a challenging situation with diminishing probability for success.

To change the trends with packaged software implementations, we first need to change paradigms. There are literally hundreds of books and publications on packaged software implementation best practices and pitfalls. Too often, we jump to the "How" before we completely understand the "What". We carve package service implementations into neat little silos and lose sight of the overall business solution. We look to process and methodology to produce business value when it is people who correctly apply methods that produce sustainable business value. Too often, we fixate on packaged software features rather than determine if packaged software drives require business results. Technology is not the answer to every business pain. Minimizing the Total Cost of Ownership in packaged software requires a partnership-partnership relationship between customers, implementation partners, and packaged software providers. Our current thinking regarding packaged software did not occur overnight, and shifting our strategies and expectations of packaged software will not change in a single meeting. However, I want to encourage you to change. Each player (Business, IT, Implementation Partner, Packaged Software Provider) has the opportunity to stretch and better support the success of their partners. Together, our combined efforts will reverse the trend and generate greater success for all.

I look forward to seeing you out in the field!

References

1. M.H. Martin, *An ERP Strategy*. Fortune, February 1998, Page. 95-97

Summary of Challenges

Challenge	Chapter	Audience
Identify up-front the decisions that customers need to make.	Chapter 1 – Focus on Business Results	Implementation Partners
Reduce alignment risk by speaking in business terms and not technical terms.	Chapter 1 – Focus on Business Results	Implementation Partners, IT
Perform a business value analysis on existing processes in order to eliminate non-value-added requirements.	Chapter 1 – Focus on Business Results	Customer
Document existing business processes to better identify organizational change.	Chapter 2 – Invest in Your Implementation Partner	Customer
Develop trust with implementation partners to foster greater, innovative, and dynamic interactions that will result in a cost reduction and accelerate implementation activities.	Chapter 2 – Invest in Your Implementation Partner	Customer
Provide training for every packaged software product that they offer. Implementation partners should be a customer advisor , recommending training classes and the appropriate sequence in which they should be taken.	Chapter 2 – Invest in Your Implementation Partner	Packaged Software Provider, Implementation Partner

Challenge	Chapter	Audience
Provide implementation questionnaires up-front to the customer before project start-up. This will increase your customer's chance for success.	Chapter 2 – Invest in Your Implementation Partner	Implementation Partners
Have a formal customer enablement process with specific milestones.	Chapter 3 – Enable the Customer to Lead During the Implementation	Implementation Partners
Promote a trusting work environment in order to foster maximum knowledge transfer.	Chapter 3 – Enable the Customer to Lead During the Implementation	Customers
Provide prototyping or "proof of concept" services in order to quickly gather business requirements.	Chapter 4 – Perform Business Solution Modeling	Implementation Partners
Business requirements should give more weight to business scenarios and not focus only on software functionality.	Chapter 4 – Perform Business Solution Modeling	Customers
Understand the customer's business model in order to lead them on the best approach (software, business process change) to address business requirements.	Chapter 4 – Perform Business Solution Modeling	Implementation Partners, IT
Provide working packaged software early in the implementation for prototyping and modeling.	Chapter 4 – Perform Business Solution Modeling	Implementation Partners, Packaged Software Providers
Must be able to support multiple implementation approaches for packaged software.	Chapter 5 – Determine the Right Implementation Approach	Implementation Partners
Reduce the "IT-Business" divide by having IT involved in business-related project activities and having Business involved in IT-related project activities.	Chapter 5 – Determine the Right Implementation Approach	IT, Business
Document existing processes to quantify organizational change.	Chapter 5 – Determine the Right Implementation Approach	Customer
Build flexibility into packaged software in order to support the different business process maturity levels.	Chapter 6 – Implement to the Current Business Maturity Level	Packaged Software Providers

Challenge	Chapter	Audience
Provide a complete set of business process models with different maturity levels represented.	Chapter 6 – Implement to the Current Business Maturity Level	Packaged Software Providers
Recommend to customers a set of packaged software features to implement, based upon the current business process maturity level.	Chapter 6 – Implement to the Current Business Maturity Level	Implementation Partners
Implementation partners need to guide their customers to ensure that there is alignment between project sponsors and end user requirements, with the executive sponsors guiding objectives and principles for utilizing packaged software.	Chapter 6 – Implement to the Current Business Maturity Level	Implementation Partners
Have a standard definition of key business requirements for a business process to analyze against the current set of customer requirements, to ensure completeness.	Chapter 7 – Minimize Customizations and Maximize Enhancements	Implementation Partner
Know the customer's business model in order to facilitate discussions with the customer in examining/evaluating business requirements.	Chapter 7 – Minimize Customizations and Maximize Enhancements	Implementation Partners
Understand the detailed software dependencies and data requirements for packaged software.	Chapter 8 – Negotiate for Success	Implementation Partners
Provide software configuration workbooks that define the table setup sequence as well as the key questions to consider before defining business values.	Chapter 9 – Have a Business Solution Architect	Implementation Partners

Challenge	Chapter	Audience
Provide functionality and implementation questionnaires to assist in gathering information. These questionnaires should be progressively elaborate—meaning that there should be a logical progression in the questions to a deeper focus in a specific area. The questionnaires should also be grouped in such a manner that allows sets of questions to be eliminated based upon the packaged software implementation scope.	Chapter 10 – Accelerate Decisions by Generating More Knowledge and less Information	Implementation Partners
Provide industry, implementation, and configuration best practices. These best practices should be formally documented and provided early in the implementation where they have the greatest benefit.	Chapter 10 – Accelerate Decisions by Generating More Knowledge and less Information	Implementation Partners

Index

F

Field readiness plan 112
Fit Gap sessions 68
functional lead 170
functional-oriented project plan
versus business process-oriented project
plan 176

G

global considerations 114, 115

H

Holistic focus
versus Silo 104

I

implementation partner
business processes 41
business process models 42, 43
complete packaged software, training 49
customer, levels 46
educating, on existing business solutions
46, 47
implications 62-64
investment, making 40
leadership styles, employing 61, 62
packaged software implementation,
questionnaires 47, 48
project orientation, conducting 48
trust, building 44, 45
implementation partner, expectations
about 49
business process maps, detailed 51, 52
business process models, predefined 50
business solution experts, certified 53
packaged software implementation,
questionnaires 52
implementation partners 184
implementation scope
about 182
COTS implementation 182
information gathering
decision-oriented approach 182

traditional approach 180
initial (simple), business solution
maturity 122
IT
or business 90, 91

J

Joint Application Development (JAD)
session 143

K

knowledge transfer plan 58

L

lean 128

M

methodologies
applying, for COTS implementations 102
for business solution implementation 90
integrating 103
selecting, factors 100
methodologies, applying for COTS
implementations
deployment strategy 112
global considerations 114, 115
organizational change management 110
project mangement 103
software development 107
methodologies, business solution
implementation
project management 20, 21
software development 20
methodologies selecting, factors
about 100
business-IT relationship and culture 101
dynamic business model 101
implementation, size 100
personnel capabilities 100
principles 101, 102
risk 100
modeling. *See* **Business solution modeling**

O

organizational change management
about 98, 110
current business model, defining 110, 111
field readiness plan 112
future business model, defining 110, 111
organizational, requirements 111

P

packaged business software 173
packaged software
advantages 192
challenges 192
packaged software changes 119, 120
packaged software implementation
business results, key drivers 31, 32
business, values 32-34
effective negotiation strategy,
developing 156
project, scope 30
traditional measures 30
packaged software implementation,
implementation partner
questionnaries 47
packaged software implementations
issues 12, 13
packaged software partner
key long-term investments, overview 161
key short-term investments,
overview 160, 161
packaged software provider, effective
negotiation strategy
utilizing 159
Phased, deployment strategy
advantages 113
attribute 114
disadvantages 113
organization-driven 114
software-driven (module/application or
set of features) 114
PMBOK 94
Professional Services Automation. *See* **PSA**
Professional Services Organization
illustration 127, 128

project control 104
project management
about 94
Business and IT, balanced project
leadership 106, 107
project control 104
risk versus reward 105
Silo versus Holistic focus 104
Project Management Body of Knowledge.
See **PMBOK**
project manager 170
project orientation
conducting, with implementation
partner 48
prototyping 143
about 69, 70
customers, challenge to 71
implementation partners, challenge to 70
requirements management, activities 69
versus modeling 72
PSA
business process maturity 122

Q

quality 128
quality management
and business process management 98-100

R

requirements-driven strategy
about 140
advantages 141
disadvantages 141
requirements, gathering
interviewing 143
Joint Application Development (JAD)
session 143
prototyping 143
use cases 143
requirements management, revisited
about 142, 143
requirements, analyzing 144
requirements, gathering 143
requirements, selecting 145
requirements, validating 144

requirements management, strategies
configuration-driven 142
requirements-driven 141
solution-driven 141
requirements, validating
business solution modeling 144
peer reviews 144
test cases 144
Return on Investment. *See* **ROI**
reward
versus risk 105
risk
versus reward 105
Robbins-Gioia Survey 10
ROI 39
ruleflow. *See* **Drools Flow**

S

sequential development
versus business process development 108
Silo
versus Holistic focus 104
software design tools 118
software development
about 107
methodologies 95
sequential development versus business
process development 108
software development, tailoring for
COTS 108, 109
software development, methodologies
Code-and-Fix 95
Crystal Family (Agile) 96
Design to Schedule 96
Design to Tools 96
Evolutionary Delivery 96
Rational Unified Process 96
Spiral 95
Waterfall 95
solution-based approach 91
solution-driven strategy
about 140
advantages 141
disadvantages 141

T

TAC 129
TCO 156
technical lead 170
Total Cost of Ownership. *See* **TCO**
traditional approach, information gathering
about 180
information, versus knowledge 181
**traditional packaged software
implementation 169-171**
Trusted Advisors Consulting. *See* **TAC**

V

value-added requirements management
about 146
business requirements, challenging 147
challenges 151
customer, leading 147
customer, listening to 146
customer, negotiating with 147
customizations 148
customizations versus enhancements 148
enhancements 148-150
risks 152

W

waterfall software development lifecycle
about 67, 68
customer reviews, validation technique 68
design phase 68
development phase 68
disadvantages 68
peer reviews, validation technique 68
planning phase 68
requirements phase 68
testing phase 68
testing, validation technique 68
validation, technique 68

 **Thank you for buying**
Maximize Your Investment: 10 Key
Strategies for Effective Packaged
Software Implementations

About Packt Publishing

Packt, pronounced 'packed', published its first book *"Mastering phpMyAdmin for Effective MySQL Management"* in April 2004 and subsequently continued to specialize in publishing highly focused books on specific technologies and solutions.

Our books and publications share the experiences of your fellow IT professionals in adapting and customizing today's systems, applications, and frameworks. Our solution based books give you the knowledge and power to customize the software and technologies you're using to get the job done. Packt books are more specific and less general than the IT books you have seen in the past. Our unique business model allows us to bring you more focused information, giving you more of what you need to know, and less of what you don't.

Packt is a modern, yet unique publishing company, which focuses on producing quality, cutting-edge books for communities of developers, administrators, and newbies alike. For more information, please visit our website: www.packtpub.com.

Writing for Packt

We welcome all inquiries from people who are interested in authoring. Book proposals should be sent to author@packtpub.com. If your book idea is still at an early stage and you would like to discuss it first before writing a formal book proposal, contact us; one of our commissioning editors will get in touch with you.

We're not just looking for published authors; if you have strong technical skills but no writing experience, our experienced editors can help you develop a writing career, or simply get some additional reward for your expertise.

SOA Patterns with BizTalk Server 2009

ISBN: 978-1-847195-00-5   Paperback: 400 pages

Implement SOA strategies for BizTalk Server solutions

1. Discusses core principles of SOA and shows them applied to BizTalk solutions

2. The most thorough examination of BizTalk and WCF integration in any available book

3. Leading insight into the new WCF SQL Server Adapter, UDDI Services version 3, and ESB Guidance 2.0

4. Loaded with examples, demo code, and screenshots, which explain how to design schemas, build WSDL-first endpoints, build loosely coupled orchestrations and, much more

SAP Business ONE Implementation

ISBN: 978-1-847196-38-5   Paperback: 320 pages

Bring the power of SAP Enterprise Resource Planning to your small-midsize business

1. Get SAP B1 up and running quickly, optimize your business, inventory, and manage your warehouse

2. Understand how to run reports and take advantage of real-time information

3. Complete an express implementation from start to finish

Please check **www.PacktPub.com** for information on our titles

Oracle SOA Suite Developer's Guide

ISBN: 978-1-847193-55-1   Paperback: 652 pages

Design and build Service-Oriented Architecture Solutions with the Oracle SOA Suite 10gR3

1. A hands-on guide to using and applying the Oracle SOA Suite in the delivery of real-world SOA applications.

2. Detailed coverage of the Oracle Service Bus, BPEL Process Manager, Web Service Manager, Rules, Human Workflow, and Business Activity Monitoring.

3. Master the best way to combine / use each of these different components in the implementation of a SOA solution.

SOA Cookbook

ISBN: 978-1-847195-48-7   Paperback: 268 pages

Master SOA process architecture, modeling, and simulation in BPEL, TIBCO's BusinessWorks, and BEA's Weblogic Integration

1. Lessons include how to model orchestration, how to build dynamic processes, how to manage state in a long-running process, and numerous others

2. BPEL tools discussed include BPEL simulator, BPEL compiler, and BPEL complexity analyzer

3. Examples in BPEL, TIBCO's BusinessWorks, BEA's Weblogic Integration

Please check **www.PacktPub.com** for information on our titles